Blackmail payoff . . .

At three o'clock we ran through the town, up the street from school, past the shops, and under the railroad bridge on North Louella.

We crossed the fields and followed along the edge of the train embankment until we reached the overpass at Eagle Road. I don't know why we hurried so much. Excitement, I guess. . . .

B.J. kept checking his watch. We were all kind of hyper. The anticipation was killing us.

"It's been fun, huh?" B.J. said. "The perfect crime bit. And we're going to pull it off just like we planned."

"I sure hope so," I said. "I just have a feeling that something is going to go wrong."

"You're out of your skull, Chad. Nothing can go wrong now." B.J. checked his watch for about the millionth time. "In five minutes when that train roars by and Patterson throws the money out the window, we're free and clear. . . ."

LETTER PERFECT

Charles P. Crawford

PUBLISHED BY POCKET BOOKS NEW YORK

POCKET BOOKS, a Simon & Schuster division of
GULF & WESTERN CORPORATION
1230 Avenue of the Americas, New York, N.Y. 10020

Published by arrangement with E. P. Dutton, a Division of
Sequoia-Elsevier Publishing Company, Inc.
Library of Congress Catalog Card Number: 77-4180

ISBN: 0-671-29945-X

First Pocket Books printing June, 1979

10 9 8 7 6 5 4 3 2 1

Trademarks registered in the United States and other countries.

Printed in the U.S.A.

to the real Chad

CHAPTER 1

I glanced at the clock. There were ten minutes left in the period. I had just started the second essay question on the *Great Expectations* exam in English. I'd really have to push to get a decent answer done in that time.

Just as I'd written my first sentence: "The growth of Pip's moral values depended a great deal on the people he encountered in the story," I felt B.J.'s eyes on my paper. It's funny, but you can always sense when someone is looking at your paper during a test. It's like a sixth sense or something. I didn't want to look over to be sure, but I did. How could I help it? Sure enough, his eyes were halfway out of his head straining to see what I was writing. I was a little angry. After all, I'd loaned B.J. my notes the night before. You wouldn't think he'd need to look at my answers too.

He gave me a feeble grin and a little shrug of his shoulders. I moved my right arm down to my side and shifted my test paper so he could see it better. What could I do? After all, a friend in need, and all that crap. You can't exactly throw away a friendship that went back to second grade over some dumb piece of paper.

I glanced toward the front of the room and met Mr. Patterson's gaze. I knew that he knew that I knew exactly what I was doing. He was smiling.

"Excuse me, children of grace," Mr. Patterson said in a loud voice and everyone looked up from their papers. "I don't mean to interrupt when time, I'm sure, is of the essence to all you snail-paced workers, but I've made an anthropological discovery. It will be a revelation to modern science and I wanted you to share in my excitement."

I heard LeeAnne Panelli giggling behind me. She chortled insanely at whatever Mr. Patterson said. I suspected that there was a hyena in her family tree.

"A new breed of man has emerged here in this very classroom," Mr. Patterson continued. "Homo binoculus."

Just about everyone laughed at that. Even I chuckled uncomfortably. He was leaning on his podium casually in his perfectly pressed, with-it clothes. His longish hair was perfectly combed. His teeth were showing white in a half smile. I had a feeling that Mr. Patterson could survive a ten-day typhoon and still look like everything was in place. Unfortunately I couldn't sit back and relax with everybody else. I had the premonition that my roof was falling in. The rafters were already creaking over my head.

"For those of you ignorant enough to think that I've just made a dirty joke, let me enlighten you. In this case, 'homo' is Latin for 'man,' not a colloquial term for sexual preferences. Indeed, 'Homo binoculus' seems to be a human subspecies that has emerged full grown beneath our very eyes. I am speaking of no one else but B.J. Masterson, who evidently has eyes on the side of his head."

Another round of laughter swept the room. The words dazzled. I looked down at my paper and saw the pencil squiggles I had been unconsciously doodling in the margin. It's never very funny to be the brunt of Mr. Patterson's sarcasm. It's only funny for the rest of the class, and they were enjoying it as usual.

"Now I know why B.J. wears that unruly shock of hair. I used to think he was trying to hide the fact that he had no ears, but now I clearly realize that it is to cover that extra set of eyes that not only sets him apart from us standard, ordinary models of the human race, but also provides him with hindsight on tests. Or should I say sidesight? Mr. Masterson and Mr. Winston, who is the source of B.J.'s inspiration, will see me after class. I'm sorry for the interruption, group. Please, continue. And do me a favor, huh? How about doing better on this test than you did on the last one. I'd like to be able to grade them with a minimum of groaning."

The laughter died out and the sound of scribbling pencils returned.

I tried to finish the last essay question, but my mind only ran in circles and I couldn't get anything organized on paper. All I could think about was the session we'd have when the ball rang. Damn, why did B.J. have to be so dumb about it?

Just as the bell clanged, Mr. Patterson said, "All right. Stop thinking. Make sure your name is at the top of the paper. Anyone who wants to be anonymous can save it for the school literary magazine where everything should be nameless. Pass your papers to the head of the row and then you're dismissed."

I got the papers from LeeAnne behind me and then passed them up to Steve Sorrell. I was in the second desk of the row. I waited until the room began to clear. Then I leaned over toward B.J.

"Thanks a lot, B.J. Why didn't you at least cheat off Missy's paper to your right? She's one of his pets. He'd never come down on her like that."

B.J. grinned. "Sorry, pal. I just like your handwriting better, I guess."

"Think he'll fail us on the test?" I asked. I was pushing for an A that term. This would blow the whole thing.

"I don't know. I hope not."

"Gentlemen, gentlemen," Mr. Patterson said. "No conspiracies, please. Come up here a second." For a first-year teacher, he sure knew all the moves.

B.J. and I stood and walked toward Mr. Patterson's desk. He was sitting on the edge of it, rumpling a disorderly pile of papers beneath his butt. No matter how neat he was about himself, his desk always looked like a tornado had hit a notebook factory.

"And, Toad—" Mr. Patterson said in a loud voice. I turned. Toad was standing by the classroom door at the back of the room, waiting for B.J. and me. "—unless you plan to be the defense attorney, I suggest you wait for your friends in the hall."

"Yes, sir," Toad said and went out into the corridor.

Mr. Patterson turned to us.

"You know, boys, there are many succesful examples of collaboration in the history of our culture. There was Rodgers and Hammerstein, and Kaufman and Hart, and some even suggest that Shakespeare couldn't hack it alone. And let's, please, not forget Laurel and Hardy, which bears a closer resemblance to the situation at hand. Before I pass judgment, does either of you have anything to say?"

You could tell Mr. Patterson was loving every minute of it.

"Listen, Mr. Patterson," B.J. said. "I wasn't cheating. I wasn't really. I already had that answer written down. I swear I did. I was only kind of checking to see if my paper agreed with Chad's. That's all."

"Admirable, B.J. A nice try, but I seem to recall having heard those same words somewhere before in my teaching career."

"And besides, Chad didn't have anything to do with it. It's not his fault he happened to be sitting next to me. I don't think it's fair to blame him too." Mr. Patterson raised one eyebrow. It was his left eyebrow. It always was. We'd seen the look before.

"Who said I was going to blame Chad too?" Mr. Patterson asked.

I breathed a sigh of relief. Thank God, I thought, and I mentally began reaching for that A again.

"Aren't you?" B.J. asked.

"Of course. I just hadn't mentioned it yet. Here's the way it stands. Collaborators should share the credit. I'm convinced that you two have come up with a superior test paper. It only seems fair that I grade both papers, average the scores, and divide by two so you both get equal credit for your work. For instance, if the two papers average out in the range of a 96, then you'll each get a 48. How's that?"

"But that's a failure on the test," I said.

5

"Astute, Chad. Very astute. But then, where would Rodgers have been without Hammerstein? Perhaps next time, you'll be a bit more circumspect in looking for answers, B.J."

"Yes, sir," B.J. said between his closed teeth. I could tell he was steaming.

"I'll see you tomorrow. We'll be starting on *Paradise Lost*. It's an appropriate time to turn over a new leaf. You may go."

B.J. and I left the room. Toad was waiting for us in the hall.

"What happened?" Toad asked. Even though I was madder than hell, I almost had to laugh. Toad's face was covered with concern, his buggy eyes almost squinted shut, and his small chin thrust forward.

"The court jester for the Marquis de Sade has struck again," B.J. said. "I wonder how he sleeps at night."

"By counting weasels," I said. "Let's get some lunch." I didn't want to talk about it.

"Yeah, but what happened?" Toad asked again as we made our way down the stairway toward the basement. He was walking backwards down the steps in front of us.

"We failed. That's all," B.J. said.

"That's all?" I said. "That's enough."

"Both of you?"

"Yeah," I said.

"Listen, Chad. I really am sorry," B.J. said. "It was dumb of me."

"Jesus," Toad said. "He failed both of you?"

"What else? The man is power crazy. He'd have made a perfect executioner," B.J. said.

6

"Both of you! That sure was dumb, B.J. Aren't you mad, Chad?"

"Well, I'm not exactly going to celebrate," I replied. "Maybe he'll let me do an extra composition to make up for it or something. Next time though, do me a favor, B.J."

"What?"

"Wear blinders."

Toad laughed.

"Shut up, why don't you," I said, and Toad turned around and led the way toward the lunchroom.

"Poor Chad," said B.J. "Pure as the driven snow." Toad laughed again.

It took B.J. and me almost fifteen minutes to get through the lunch line. It's a masterpiece of inefficiency and by the time we had gotten to the cafeteria, we were all the way at the end. We didn't see anyone further ahead of us who would let us butt in.

Luckily Toad had brought his lunch and had saved us a table. B.J. and I crossed the lunchroom and sat down with him.

I had gotten the federal lunch. Pizza, with a four-inch crust and a scum of tomato catsup on top, potato chips, milk, and cake for dessert. One of these days someone is going to drop over from carbohydrate shock. B.J. had his usual: orangeade, two soft pretzels, and two ice cream sandwiches.

Toad was already half through his sandwich. I was almost afraid to ask. I didn't have to. B.J. asked for me.

"What do you have today?"

"Rice Krispies and banana on rye," Toad said.

I almost got up and left, but it was no worse than normal. The day before, Toad's sandwich had been a chocolate pudding sandwich on toast. It had oozed out the sides while he ate it.

"There's something I've always wanted to know about your sandwiches, Toad," B.J. said.

"What's that?"

"Does your mother make them for you?"

"Hell, no. I make them myself. Mom always make me sandwiches I don't like."

"Like ham and cheese?" I asked.

"Yeah. And who wants to eat ham and cheese when you can have something great like Rice Krispies," he said and grinned. "The only trouble with today's sandwich is that it was all done snap, crackle, and popping before the second period. Two hundred and seven snaps, four hundred and seventy crackles, and thirteen pops, to be exact. A new world's record."

I laughed and felt better. Besides eating the world's strangest sandwiches, Toad is a game-o-maniac. He's forever making up weird contests and things. Like one rainy Saturday, we were sitting around Toad's house and he got the bright idea of seeing how long each of us could balance on a brick turned long way up. B.J. and I sat around watching him standing on that dumb brick for two hours and four minutes. Then he fell off. Probably from exhaustion. When he said, "Okay, who's next?" we laughed our heads off. I think his life's ambition is to break every one of the Guinness World Records. You give Toad the idea for a game and nothing else in the world matters until the game is over and he's won.

"I tell you," B.J. said, "one of these days, Patterson's going to go a little too far. God, he makes me mad sometimes."

8

"Too bad about the test," Toad said. "You should have known better. That man doesn't let anything slip past his eyes."

"I know. But I really did have the answer already written. I was telling him the truth. It was the same answer as yours anyway, Chad."

"Would you have changed it if it had been different?" I asked.

"I don't know," B.J. said. "But I didn't have to. It was right all along. It isn't fair."

"The only thing that isn't fair is you happened to get caught," Toad said.

"Yeah, but he didn't have to do a job on us in front of everyone."

"And failing Chad too, I mean, Jesus," Toad said.

"He saw me shove the paper toward B.J.," I said.

"You didn't have to," B.J. said. "You could have tucked it under your armpit safely out of sight instead of leaving it out in fully view to tempt my beady blues."

"No, I couldn't have, B.J. You know it too. If I see you looking at my paper, there's nothing else I can do but let you see it."

B.J. reached over and patted my shoulder. "That's my buddy," he said. "I knew I kept you around for some reason." His smile made me smile too.

"Anyway, you know Mr. Patterson," I said. "That's his thing. He loves to play the audience for all it's worth. I didn't see you not laughing the other day when he made Beth put the gum on the end of her nose for the whole period."

"Well, that really was funny," B.J. said. "The wad was so big she looked like a clown."

"And don't forget the time he made Sam lick a whole book of green stamps and paste them in one at a time for throwing spit balls," Toad said. "And you're lucky if everybody doesn't call you 'Homo binoculus' for the next few weeks. The best thing to do in Mr. Patterson's class is to be as inconspicuous as possible."

"Like you?" B.J. said.

"Exactly like I do. You haven't seen him making a fool out of me in front of everyone, have you? I figure it's a challenge to make it through the whole year without being called out once by Mr. Patterson."

"Your trouble is, Toad, you're going to go through your whole life being inconspicuous unless you can get a job at the circus," B.J. said.

"That's not true. There's no reason to get pissed off at Toad," I said.

"Touchy, touchy," B.J. said. "Well, the whole thing's a waste. I don't know why we're spending half our life studying crap like *Great Expectations* anyway. What good is it? Name me one thing this year that will do us any good when we get out of this dump. Just one thing."

"There was the sex education unit in biology," Toad suggested.

"Dreamer," B.J. said. "That's no more practical for you than studying the Punic Wars. Anyone who eats Rice Krispies in their sandwich is going to be a virgin until they're fifty."

"How about algebra?" I suggested. "That's practical."

"Like hell I can just see myself balancing my checkbook by going $a^2 + b^2 = c^2$. You haven't convinced me yet."

"Well, that's what college is for," I said.

"Don't believe it. I have a brother in college right

now. The courses he's taking are more useless than ours. Whoever heard of making a living off the Transcendentalism in Colonial American Literature or Medieval Art 301–302. You don't find out what the world's like until graduate school—law school or something—and you're old by then."

"Oh, I don't know, B.J.," I said. "It seems to me that there are a lot of things that are good to know even though you may never use them much."

"I can't buy it, Chad. We should be learning important things, things we can use. Like how to lie if you want to be a politician or how to make it with the producer if you want to be in the movies or how to cheat on your income tax if you want to be just about anybody."

"Who turned him on?" Toad asked.

I shrugged. B.J. smiled.

"Seriously, you guys. I'm not just kidding. Don't you feel like you've spent all these years being talked at in a classroom and you're no better off than you were when you started kindergarten?"

"Not especially," I said. When B.J. got wound up, there was no way of shutting him up. Even when we were little kids, we'd all get caught up in B.J.'s crazy schemes. Like the time we tried to bring his uncle's cow in for show-and-tell in second grade. Or the time we sold lemonade on the street corner when we were nine. Only B.J. suggested we use salt instead of sugar so people would get thirstier and thirstier and end up buying more. Instead we had a neighborhood full of stomachaches. B.J.'s ideas were always infectious, like the measles, only more fun.

"Take crime, for instance. You have to learn all kinds of skills to be a criminal. You just don't walk

11

out and rob a bank for the first time without learning a lot first. And get away with it, I mean. You have to know practical stuff, like how to drive a car, how to write concise, clear notes to pass to the teller, how to count up all the cash once you've got it. Crime is totally interdisciplinary. That's the kind of thing we should be learning in school. Stuff you can use once you get out in that world out there."

Toad almost choked on a Rice Krispie, he was laughing so hard. It was a funny idea.

"I can just see old Miss Feinstein teaching an elective course in getaways," I said.

"And how about Mr. Robbins, in gym, training us in jumping from fire escapes and entering second-floor windows. It would be just as challenging as push-ups," Toad put in.

"In art we could learn how to cut out and paste letters from the newspaper for ransom notes. Things like that," B.J. said. "If you're going to do it, you might as well do it artistically."

"How about learning to sew our own masks and hoods in home ec," Toad added.

"And in history we can study the development of the Mafia," I said.

"Now you're talking. That's a real school for you. None of this *Great Expectations* crap. Just the nitty-gritty of the real world."

"I tell you what they can teach you to do with this pizza," I said. I could feel it settling like a lump in my stomach. "You could tie it on the leg of someone you wanted to wipe out and it would be just as efficient as a block of concrete. Two-ton pizza boots."

"For Mr. Patterson." B.J. said. "Ten fathoms down."

12

"What do you say we bring it up at the student council advisory meeting," Toad said. "They're always looking for curriculum suggestions."

All of a sudden B.J.'s eyes lit up. He smashed his open palm down on the table, spilling what was left of my milk. Toad's bread crusts hopped a good half foot.

"Aha," he said and pointed his index finger toward the ceiling. "Listen, you guys, have I got an idea!"

I groaned. I'd listened to some of B.J.'s ideas before.

"No, listen." He was grinning maniacally. "A forreal idea. We lead a pretty dull life, right? Up at seven, seven hours of classes, home for homework and it's getting us nowhere. Just for fun, you know, for kicks, let's plan a perfect crime. How's that for an inspiration?"

I laughed, even though I didn't think B.J. was trying to be funny anymore.

"No, really. How's that, huh? The perfect crime! It's just the kind of thing that active young minds like ours need. Our brains will turn to jelly if we don't do something special to keep them going."

"For real?" Toad asked. The possibility of a game was turning him on. I could see him beginning to scritch in his seat already.

"Not for real, idiot. Just for the mental exercise. And nothing big. We're not exactly pros. But think how much fun it would be to plan it all out, even if we don't go through with anything. Jesus, the perfect crime!"

"But how do we know it's perfect if we don't go through with it?" I asked.

"That's beside the point. Don't quibble, Chad.

13

How's it sound, Toad? You two game? Design the perfect crime, just for the hell of it."

"Sounds more exciting than math homework," I said.

"I'll be the brains behind the operation, Chad can be the getaway man and, Toad, you can be the muscle. You with me?"

"Sure," Toad said. "The three musketeers." He stabbed at me with his Tastykake.

"It sounds funny," I said.

"Funny? Hell, it's hilarious. It's the best idea I've had in years, if I do say so myself. This will really train our minds. We'll have to put our heads together on everything."

"I've watched lots of television cop shows," Toad said. "I know what doesn't work."

"Our problem is figuring out something that does. All we have to do is decide on what kind of crime we want it to be."

"Rape," Toad said.

B.J. put down his second ice cream sandwich. "Wouldn't you know it. Junior sex fiend wants to plan a rape. Anyone special?"

"How about Roxanne Spiese?" Toad suggested.

"You don't have to rape her," B.J. replied. "Give her five bucks and she'd do it on the gym mats."

"Really?" Toad said.

"Try it," I suggested. "How about kidnapping? I've got a little sister I'd be happy to donate. A million dollars in ransom."

"Can your father afford that? Wow!" Toad said.

"Of course he can't afford that," I said. "That's the idea."

"We can't just jump into this thing," B.J. said. "We've got to learn the ropes first. Before we decide on the crime, maybe we should have a period of training."

"Criminal calisthenics," I said.

"Exactly. I tell you what. Just so we all can prove our skill at this kind of stuff, how about a little assignment for us."

"Like what?"

"Sometime before three o'clock tomorrow, each of us has to pull off some sort of harmless crime, a joke or something, around school and get away with it. That will prove where our talents lie."

"Or don't lie."

"Okay?"

"You mean actually do something? I think we were going to go beyond the planning stage," I said.

"Not a crime. Just a joke on somebody around school. Like a practical joke or something. Just make sure you cover your tracks is all. If you can't make it and you get caught, then we know that we'd never be able to plan a real crime. How's it sound?"

"Okay by me," I said. I was already trying to think of something that would work.

"And none of us will know what the other is going to do," B.J. said. "We'll meet after school tomorrow and see if we can figure out what each of the jokes was. If you can get away with it." B.J. loved dropping that kind of challenge.

"Don't worry. I will," Toad said. He was leaning forward over his bread crusts. He never does eat his crusts.

"I've got an idea already," I said. It was good to get my mind off the hassle in English class.

"Good," B.J. said. "And no one squeals on anyone else. Right?"

"Of course not," I said.

"One for all and all for one, like you said," Toad replied.

We slapped each other's hands on it. The three of us together as usual. This was exactly B.J.'s kind of thing.

"Let's go," I said. "We'll be late for science."

We put our trays back and threw away the trash. We passed Mr. Patterson at the door of the cafeteria.

"Aha," he said. "The Three Stooges: Larry, Curly, and Mo Binoculus. Have a pleasant afternoon, boys."

"We will," B.J. said. Halfway down the hall, under his breath he added, "You bastard."

CHAPTER 2

I got to school early the next morning. I had some groundwork to do.

I ditched my jacket in my locker outside Mr. Patterson's room on the third floor. The halls were almost deserted before eight. None of the buses had arrived yet. I was a walker. It was kind of creepy in the empty halls.

I grabbed two overdue books and went down to the school library. It was always open for a half hour before homeroom started. There were a few kids there, probably finishing up last minute research papers due that day. I crossed to the desk and laid the books on the counter.

The librarian, Mrs. Folger, flipped to the back cover where the due-date was listed, did a split second of mental math, and declared, "Twenty-four cents due, Chad."

I scrounged some coins from my pocket and gave her a quarter.

"Keep the change," I said. "I'm amazingly generous before nine in the morning."

"Sweet of you, Chad," she said. "All the fines go toward more book purchases, you know. Sometimes

I feel you students think the money goes into my own pocket."

The idea of Mrs. Folger embezzling from the library fine drawer almost made me laugh out loud.

"I can't see you as the criminal type, Mrs. Folger," I said.

"I do have an honest face, don't I? Thanks for the books, Chad. Save yourself a few cents and get them back on time in the future."

"Okay," I said.

I turned from the desk and went into the book stacks. I already felt guilty about what I was going to do, but I had racked my brains all night trying to think of something good to pull that would impress Toad and B.J. It was the only thing I could think of. Besides, it wouldn't do any real damage. There are always a few hundred library aides hanging around with nothing much to do except play with the card catalog. Let them pick the books up. It's just that I did kind of like Mrs. Folger and I didn't want to cause her that much trouble.

I found the 360 section of non-fiction. I thought it would be appropriate. It was the section on crime. I checked to see if Mrs. Folger was watching, but there was no one in sight. I started at the bottom shelf and carefully removed two of the little metal bolts that held up the adjustable wooden shelves. I had it all figured out. If I removed two of the four supports, the front left one and the back right one, the shelf would be precariously balanced. The next time a book was returned to the shelf, the whole shelf would go, spilling books out into the aisle. If the person was lucky, and put a book on the top shelf, I had calculated that, like a domino effect, all the book shelves below would go too.

I only did one set of shelves, four altogether. I made sure that none of the shelves I'd booby trapped were over waist level. I didn't want anyone getting clunked on the head by a falling book. Then I grabbed a book on police procedure. I made sure that all the shelves were in perfect balance. They were, so I returned to the check-out desk.

"Oh, interested in being a policeman?" Mr. Folger said as I placed the book on the counter.

"Not really. It just looked like an interesting book."

"Well, I hope you enjoy it," she said and passed it back to me. I gave her a winning Chad Winston smile and headed for the door. I wanted to be far away when the shelves fell in.

I went back up toward my homeroom on the third floor. There were only five minutes left until the bell. When I saw the crowd at the end of the hallway, I knew that either Toad or B.J. had been to work early too.

Outside the science rooms on the third floor, there is a row of stuffed heads of African animals. Antelopes and things. Relics from some great white hunter of the forties who had donated them to the school. They were moth-eaten and forlorn by now and a grim reminder of a less ecological age. But they remained there, year after year, silently gazing down with marble eyes at the life of the school below.

As I got closer, I could see what had drawn the crowd. Someone had taken a bra and put it on the warthog's head like a blindfold. The white cups stood out over the warthog's snout and the straps were snapped behind the ears. I stood there with the

19

crowd and joined in the laughter, trying to figure whether it was Toad's or B.J.'s handiwork.

"Make way, make way," a voice said and I turned. Miss vanderPoole, another English teacher, was dragging a chair behind her along the hall. The crowd parted and let her through. She positioned the chair beneath the head.

She turned toward the group and said, "Funny, huh? Well, I think so too. But I think it would be a good idea to get it down or none of us will make it to homeroom on time. Who's going to be a gentleman and get up on this chair and unsnap the thing?"

Nobody volunteered.

"How about you, Louie?" Miss vanderPoole asked, pointing to Louie Schwartz, the class' champion make-out artist.

"Ah, Miss vanderPoole, I don't know how to get one of those things off," he said.

Everyone laughed.

"Don't believe it," Tom Brolin yelled. "He practices at home. Ties a bra around the banister and he's got it down to fourteen seconds."

"I wouldn't be surprised," Miss vanderPoole said. She was playing it pretty smooth. I have to give her credit for that. "How about you, Tom?"

"Sure," Tom said and climbed up on the chair. He reached above him, standing on his toes, and just managed to stretch enough to reach the snap over the ears. He gave it a flick on his fingers and the bra slipped to the ground, ten feet below.

Everyone cheered and Tom clasped his hands over his head like a prizefighter.

"Whose is it?" Miss vanderPoole asked. "Anyone want to claim it?"

"Put it in the lost and found," Louie suggested.

Tom jumped off the chair and grabbed the bra from the floor. He held it from his hand like a trophy.

"Let me have it, Tom," Mis vanderPoole said. "I'll put it in a safe place. Well out of sight. Thanks for your help. Now everybody get to homeroom. The bell's just about to ring."

Miss vanderPoole slung the bra over her arm and returned to her room, dragging the chair behind her. The crowd broke up and wandered off to lockers and classrooms.

I didn't see Toad or B.J. until fourth period when we had English together. The first two periods I had electives—art and gym—and neither Toad nor B.J. were in either of my sections there. Third period was math. I was in a special seminar kind of setup so I wasn't with the other two there either. But we had English together and after lunch, we were in the same science and history sections.

I kept wondering all morning long whether the book shelves had fallen in yet. Sometimes I wished that my little plan hadn't come off and other times I wished I'd be there to see the shelves collapse.

My question was answered outside Mr. Patterson's room. Toad and B.J. were waiting in the hall for me.

"The library bit must have been yours," B.J. said. "No one else could have been so rotten."

"You should have seen it," Toad said. "I was in there first period for elective study hall. I thought the whole building was falling in."

"Yeah, it was me," I said. "Who tripped the shelves?"

"You wouldn't believe it. It was Fred Stevenson."

Fred was the class jock. A big football type. "He went over to the stacks to get something. It surprised me. I didn't know he could read. You should have told me about the shelves so I could have kept an eye on it. I didn't see it actually happen," Toad said. "Anyway there was this tremendous crash and everybody rushed to see. Fred was standing there up to his knees in books. He's so dumb. He was looking at his hands like he didn't know his own strength or something. Like he'd done it all by himself.

"Mrs. Folger ran over. Fred said, 'Gee, sorry, Miss Folger. I didn't mean to do it. I'll help you pick them up.' I don't think Mrs. Folger was fooled for a minute. She said, 'It's not your fault, Frederick,' and we all pitched in to get the shelves back together. Mrs. Folger had to go back to her office to get extra shelf supports. What did you do with the ones you removed?"

"I put them behind the books on the next shelf over," I said.

"Very wise," B.J. said. "No way you can get caught with the evidence that way. You have real potential."

"Thanks. Shucks, guys, it was nothing." I lowered my head in mock humility. "But how about the bra? Was that you or Toad? It was one of the funniest things I've ever seen."

"Yours truly," Toad said and gave a little bow. "I thought it was pretty clever myself."

"Where'd you get the bra?" I asked.

"My sister. She'll never miss it. She hardly ever wears them anymore."

"I wish I'd been there," B.J. said. "I heard it was on the warthog."

22

"Yeah. It was the ugliest head there."

"You should have put it on the zebra."

"You're lucky you weren't caught," I said. "How'd you get it hooked behind the ears?"

"I stole a stepladder from the janitor's closet down the hall. It only took me a second."

B.J. shook his head and laughed. "What courage."

"It was no sweat. I had an alibi all ready. If someone caught me with the ladder, I was just going to say that the janitor asked me to bring it to him downstairs to change a light bulb."

"How would you have explained the bra? I don't think the janitor usually wears one."

"Yeah. Well, I hadn't exactly thought about that."

"What about you, B.J.? Have you pulled off your trick yet?" I asked.

"Coming up, guys. Stay tuned during Mr. Patterson's class. I guarantee that all hell will break loose."

"What is it?" Toad asked.

"Wait and see. Let's get going."

We went into Mr. Patterson's classroom. He was up front by the desk talking with a couple of girls. They always clustered around him like he was some sort of god or something. He had them laughing as usual with his sarcastic little jokes. I went to my desk, but B.J. went on by his seat and took out a pencil. I kept my eye on him, wondering what he was up to. He went over to the windows and began sharpening his pencil. He gave a quick glance toward the front of the room. Mr. Patterson was still talking to the girls, playing it cool. I saw B.J. take a plastic bag out of his pocket, open it, and dribble its contents into the grate of the ventilation system, the hot-air blower that is under the windows. It's supposed to keep the room temperature at a constant rate, but it always seems to blow out hot air in June and freezing air in February.

B.J. finished sharpening his pencil and returned to his seat next to me. He looked pleased with himself. He gave a small nod and dropped into his chair.

I turned back and looked at Toad, who was in his seat toward the back of the rom, by the door. Toad shrugged. He didn't know what was going on either. I shook my head back at him.

Mr. Patterson shooed the girls to their seats and took his customary position at the front of the room, one of his legs casually slung over the edge of his desk. The room quieted. You always wondered whether we'd all make it through the hour with everyone escaping his sarcastic little games. It was almost dull when the bell rang and no one had been verbally keel-hauled. "Sally, why don't you shut your mouth for a moment so I can see the back of the room," or "Frank, why don't you have your orthodontist permanently wire your mouth shut," or "You don't have your homework? If it was anything like yesterday's, it's probably just as well." Little goodies like that.

"Good morning, class. Any old business before we start on the new?"

LeeAnne raised her hand. I knew exactly what she was going to ask. She does it every time we have a test or a quiz even.

"Yes?" Mr. Patterson said.

"Do you have our tests graded from yesterday yet, Mr. Patterson?"

"LeeAnne, I'm shocked. Don't tell me that you're concerned with grades too? Doesn't anyone just learn for the pleasure of it anymore?" He gave his superior grin. "Well, as a matter of fact, I don't have them done. It seems that one of my sins is the sin of sloth. And speaking of sin, you'll all be glad to know that sin is the topic we will be exploring during the next few weeks."

I could see B.J. out of the corner of my eye. He had settled back in his seat.

"Toad, I can see from your leer that the topic is of interest to you. Unfortunately, little of what we'll be reading is titillating. That means dirty, Toad."

Toad gave a sheepish smile.

The whirr of the hot-air blower droned on below the level of Mr. Patterson's voice.

"John Milton wrote Paradise Lost in 1667. That's before you were born. It's considered one of the golden oldies of English literature which means that even if you don't like it, you'll appreciate it. Everybody turn to the opening passages on page 346 in literature anthology."

There was shuffling of papers as the class pulled out the books. The anthology weighed about three thousand pounds and even on days when we weren't going to use it, Mr. Patterson insisted we bring it to class. Sometimes it seemed as if it was becoming permanently attached to my arm, like a giant wart.

Just over the sound of rustling pages, I could hear a few people sitting in the row of seats by the windows start sniffling.

"Unfortunately, gang, our anthology only includes selections from the poem, so we'll have to do the best we can with what's available. I'll fill in the good parts as we go along."

The sniffling got louder and, even though I was sitting three rows from the window, I got a whiff of a strong, unpleasant odor.

"Milton said in *Paradise Lost* that he was going to 'justify the ways of God to man!'" Mr. Patterson continued.

The smell got stronger and more unpleasant. I glanced sideways at B.J. He was just sitting there in his seat with a grin still plastered all over his face.

"Now you've got to admit old Milton didn't have any trouble with modesty. I mean, when someone sits down at the typewriter and decides he's going to whip off a twelve-book epic poem explaining what God's all about, he doesn't suffer from an inferiority complex. Before we start reading the first section, though, I would request that the people by the window put a damper on their sinuses. It seems unfair to Milton to accompany his blank verse with a nasal chorus."

Rachel Sadlawn, who sits right next to the air blower, raised her hand.

"Yes, Rachel. Do you want a Kleenex?"

"No, Mr. Patterson. Something smells pretty bad over here."

"I beg your pardon?"

"There's something on this side of the room that's stinking everything up."

"All right, which of you guys just came from the gym?" Mr. Patterson said and got his usual laugh. Most of the class was so conditioned that even when Mr. Patterson cracked a joke that wasn't funny, people still laughed.

He put his book down on his desk and strolled

over toward Rachel. I could really smell it now too: a raunchy smell, really bad, like someone had barfed into a hot tire.

Mr. Patterson pulled up short next to Rachel. His nose was going like a rabbit's.

"I see what you mean," he said, still trying to joke the smell away.

"I think something died in your ventilator," Rachel said.

The smell was spreading fast. Even the kids further away from the windows were beginning to gasp.

I leaned over to B.J. "What is it?" I asked. "You do that?"

B.J. whispered back, "Cat food and sour milk."

"May I sit somewhere else?" Rachel asked.

"Sure, sure," Mr. Patterson said. "This whole row, move to the other side of the room. Let me see if I can tell what's in there."

Mr. Patterson looked down into the grid of the air blower. He had to hold his nose. The smell was being blown right up into his face. He was gasping through his mouth like a beached fish.

"I can't imagine what it is," he said. "I can't see anything."

"It's getting worse, Mr. Patterson," someone in the second row from the windows said.

"That's the truth," Mr. Patterson said, waving his hand in front of his face.

"I think I'm going to be sick," Rachel said.

"Then get out of here," Mr. Patterson yelled. "We don't need any more excitement. Sally, take Rachel into the girls' room. Or down to the nurse if she wants."

"Do we need a note?" Sally asked.

"Of course. But go without one. Please, get her out of this room."

Sally and Rachel sprinted for the door.

Mr. Patterson stalked back to his desk. The smell had spread throughout the room now. I tried to breathe through my shirt sleeve to filter the odor but it didn't work very well.

LeeAnne took out a spray bottle of cheap perfume and sprayed the air around her.

"Maybe this will help, Mr. Patterson," she said.

"That'll kill us all," Mr. Patterson snapped. Things were getting away from him and you could see that he didn't like it. The control was slipping through his hands. Not even sarcasm could cut the smell of B.J.'s concoction.

"What would Milton have done in a case like this?" B.J. whispered. I laughed into my sleeve.

Mr. Patterson went to the back of the room and picked the intercom phone off its hook on the wall.

LeeAnne gave a few more squirts of perfume and then began to giggle. She tried to stop herself but she couldn't. I started chuckling too. Pretty soon everyone in the room was trying to stifle their laughter.

"Listen, this is Mr. Patterson in Room 324," he said into the phone. "Will you send a janitor up here with a screwdriver? There's something in the ventilator and we need the lid removed to clean it out. Thanks."

Mr. Patterson returned the received to the cradle and swung around toward us. I could tell from his face that he was angry.

"What's so funny?" he asked. That made LeeAnne laugh a little harder. The laughter was rising up like spring water from all over the room.

"I don't know who put what in the ventilator, but

I'm going to find out," he shouted. "How does this make me look, huh? Sending for a janitor to help?"

LeeAnne covered her mouth and it sounded like she was hiccupping.

Mr. Patterson crossed back to the front of the room in five quick strides. He sat back on the edge of his desk trying to keep his cool. The smell was unbelievable now. It poured out of the air system in thick waves.

"All right. Everybody listen. I'm going to dismiss the class. I want you all to go down to the student commons and wait for the lunch hour bell," he said in a cold, quiet voice. I could hear a hint of the shakes beneath the surface. "If I hear that anyone is wandering around the hall disturbing other classes, you've had it. To make up the work that some clown has prevented us from doing today, I want each and every one of you to read the first book of *Paradise Lost* tonight. You'll have a quiz on it Monday."

We started to gather our books together. It was getting hard to breathe.

"And I want anyone who has any information about who played this little prank today to tell me in private. Understood?"

A few kids nodded their heads. I must say, I was surprised to see him so angry. I'd never seen him shook up before.

"Dismissed!"

We rushed for the door. It was like a stampede as bodies crammed into the doorway.

The janitor was just entering the room. "Jesus," he said, "what stinks?"

The class hurried down the hall to the stairs. LeeAnne was spraying a cloud of perfume behind her. It must have been called Eau de Armpit. I think I preferred the cat food.

"I don't believe you did that," Toad said to B.J. at the head of the stairs.

"Why?"

"I never thought I'd see the day when Mr. Patterson lost his cool."

"After yesterday, he deserved it," B.J. said.

"It warmed my heart," I said. "We all pass the test, I guess."

"And now we're ready for Training Test Number Two," B.J. said. "We've only just begun." He jumped down the stairs two at a time. Toad and I ran behind him. We were all flying pretty high over our first successes. It's fun to win alone, but even more fun with the three of us. We always seemed to share our victories.

We raced into the commons and sat on the graffiti-marked furniture. No matter how often they reupholstered it, it took about two weeks until the tears began to appear. I don't quite understand the kick of ripping up cloth with ballpoint pens. The rest of the class sat around in small groups laughing and joking. It was great to have the free time just to mess around.

"What the hell was it?" Toad asked. "It was incredible."

"It was cat food and sour milk mixed together," B.J. said. "I slipped some into the blower before the period started. I put it in a plastic bag on top of our furnace at home all last night just to be sure it would be totally foul."

"Jeez, hot cat food. That's disgusting," Toad said. "You're a genius."

"So what's Training Test Number Two?" I asked. I was itching to get on to the next round.

"I don't think we're ready to plan the perfect crime yet," B.J. replied. "We need some more practice at little stuff. Right?"

"Right," Toad said.

"Either of you guys doing anything tonight?"

"I'm free," I said.

"I can get out. What's up?"

"Well, we'll get together at, say, seven o'clock at the center corner of Louella. And we'll just mess around. Chad's in charge of entertainment. Toad, you're in charge of food. And I'm in charge of drink. Okay?"

"Fine," I said. "So what's so special about that? We always mess around on Friday nights."

"But tonight, everything has to be free. You'll have to be inventive. Each of us has to come up with a way to treat the rest to something for free. That should give us a little mental exercise."

"I'm food?" Toad asked.

"Yeah. And Chad's entertainment. You game?"

"Hell, sure," I said. "Seven o'clock on the main corner?"

"Yeah. It's all settled then. No backing out," B.J. said.

"Chad, can I borrow your milk carton when you're done with it at lunch?" Toad asked.

"Sure. What for?"

Toad just smiled.

Then Mr. Boughman, the assistant principal, walked into the commons. He pulled a quick halt at the door, obviously surprised to see the room full of kids during class time.

"Where are you students supposed to be right now?" he asked.

"It's okay, Mr. Boughman," LeeAnne piped up. "We're supposed to be here."

"Mr. Patterson told us to come here," B.J. said. "He's not having class today."

"Oh? Is that so?" Mr. Boughman's eyebrows just about rose to touch his receding hairline. "And where is Mr. Patterson?"

"I think he's in his room, sir," B.J. said.

"I don't want any of you leaving here to wander the halls or get to lunch early. Wait for the bell."

"Yes, Mr. Boughman," LeeAnne said.

Mr. Boughman turned through the door and started quickly up the steps. I put my money on it that he was headed for the third floor. Mr. Patterson's room, to be exact.

We all went back to passing the time until lunch. We left just two minutes before the bell. Just to make sure we were at the head of the line.

I spent all afternoon going over the entertainment possibilities. The options were limited, to say the least. And when I had to figure out how to provide it for free, I was really stumped for a while.

First I thought of bowling. We do that every once in a while on Friday nights. We hitch a ride up to the Devon Lanes and bowl some games, but I couldn't think of any way to get us a few for free. There was just no way we could get the shoes and score pad and the whole bit without paying. It was a shame there wasn't a dance going on either. I knew I could con the ticket taker at the door to slip the three of us in for free, but the next dance was in two weeks so that didn't do me any good. I hadn't heard of any party that we could crash.

So I was left with the last and usual alternative: the movies.

It was cold and raw and felt like snow. The wind whipped along Lancaster Avenue and I pulled my neck down into my ski parka as far as I could. I felt like a frozen turtle.

I was waiting at the corner by seven o'clock. I stood there looking at the dumb old-lady dresses that were in the window of the dress shop there. I didn't have to wait long though. Toad and B.J. arrived together, up Lancaster from the east, pushed along by the wind.

I waved and they waved back.

"The gruesome threesome meets again," Toad said, too loudly, into the night air. "What are the plans? Somewhere warm, I hope."

"How about the movies?" I asked. The movie theater, the Louella, a refurbished relic from the thirties, slung its ornate marquee over the street on the opposite corner.

"Fine," B.J. said. "I didn't bring any money with me though. You remember the deal, right?"

"Of course. I've got it all figured out, I think. Follow me."

We crossed at the walk light to the opposite corner. The ticket booth for the movie was a few store fronts down, past a jeweler and a card shop and a camera store. But instead of going that way, I led B.J. and Toad up the other street, past a barber shop and a gift shop. There was an alley there, which led along the side of the store to what were the exit doors of the movie theater. I knew where

33

they were because when I was a little kid at the Saturday matinees, we would go out that way to beat the crowds to the ice cream counter at Rexall's.

We walked down the alley, checking to make sure that no one saw us enter. The alley looked like it was just a dead end, but if you grabbed a sharp left behind the gift shop, a short walkway ended in a pair of fire doors.

"Jeez, I never knew these were here," Toad said. "And I've lived in Louella for five years."

"You have to be a real old-timer to know about this," I said. I'd lived in Louella all my life. In fact, my great grandfather had run a general store here back in the eighteen hundreds.

"I always wondered where those exit doors led to," B.J. said, "but I never bothered to find out. Where's the key?"

I pulled a screwdriver out of my jacket pocket. I'd never tried this before, so I didn't know whether it was going to work or not. The problem with the exit doors was they were locked from the outside and didn't have any handles. They were the push-bar type and the inside and I figured that I could get the screwdriver between the two doors, push the latch in, and get enough of a finger hold to pull the door open.

"Listen," I said. "It's pretty dark out here so there shouldn't be a problem with letting light into the theater, but do me a favor, let's make sure we hustle." My hands were shaking a little, partly from the cold and partly from the excitement. I pictured us working our butts off getting the door open and just as we did the manager would be standing on the other side, smiling, offering us a one-way trip back up the alley.

Toad got his skinny fingers part way between the doors while I pried at the latch. It slipped back, easily, and Toad got the door about an inch open. Then B.J. slipped his hand in the opening, I put the screwdriver back into the pocket, and we eased the door open another few inches.

The movie soundtrack blasted out at us, guns and screaming. Toad and I ducked under B.J.'s arm and slipped into the dark theater. B.J. followed and the door swung shut with a soft thud behind us. We kept low and moved a few rows up the aisle and grabbed for three empty seats.

I looked behind me. The theater wasn't very full. Everyone's attention was directed to the screen. I didn't see any ushers. The Louella Movie Theater isn't exactly known for its number of ushers. It's the kind of place where they let little old ladies crawl down the aisle in the dark to look for their own seats. As far as I knew, no one had spotted our illegal entry and I began to breathe a little more easily. The warmth felt good, and I shrugged my parka off and settled down to watch the flick.

"Way to go," B.J. said. "Done like a pro. You just saved us each a few dollars. I'm in your debt forever."

"Nothing to it," I whispered back. "Like stealing candy from a baby."

"How original," Toad said.

"You sound like Mr. Patterson," I said back.

"Shut up, both of you, this is good."

So we watched the movie. It wasn't so good, as it turned out. Actually, it was a pretty crappy film. Some sort of heist thing called *Crooked Millions* or something. There were a few funny lines and a good twist at the end, though. The hero, who was a cat burglar, had this whole thing planned about stealing a million in jewels during a party in a fancy penthouse apartment. He dropped the bag of diamonds down a trash chute to this girl friend who was waiting in the basement. But she ended up grabbing the wrong garbage bag and the real diamonds got churned up in a trash truck and dumped into the East River.

Toad liked it pretty much. He even likes watching the big hamburgers on the screen during intermission at the drive-in. But, as I said, I thought the whole thing was pretty dumb.

When the movie was over, we left the theater by the normal route. It was dark and cold out on the sidewalk and was starting to snow. The bank clock across the street said nine-fifteen.

"I'm in charge of food," Toad said. "Anyone hungry?"

"Sure am," I said. "You didn't bring along any of those weirdo sandwiches for us, did you?"

"No way. We're going out to eat. In style. How about the diner?"

"Fine," B.J. said.

We went up the stairs, through the little lobby with its stores and the Presbyterian Church. Down at the end of the next block, of the one-block shopping street, across from the Farmer's Market, was the Louella Diner, our local greasy spoon.

We went up the stairs, through the little lobby with its cigarette and candy machines, and into the diner itself. Inside it smelled like ten tons of hamburger had been marooned on a tropical island for a month without refrigeration. I don't know why the Board of Health hasn't closed the diner down except maybe every time they send a representative to test the food, he dies of ptomaine poisoning. I think they scrape the grease off the ceiling every week to use over again. But they make the best French fries for miles, hot, crispy, and with plenty of salt.

We sat down at one of the booths. There was a glass sugar pourer on the table, salt and pepper shakers, a plastic catsup squeeze bottle that was all clotted around the edge, and a sticky island of dried Coke. There was also a long-distance jukebox selector, but one ever bothered to flip through the offerings because all they had was golden hits of the nineteen forties played on the electric organ and accordion.

The waitress came over. She wore a rumpled white uniform and had a tag that said MARGE. Her name wasn't Marge though. We all knew her from going to the diner after the movies all the time. Her real name was Florence.

"What'll it be, kids?" she asked.

I looked at Toad. After all, he was in charge of food.

"Three hamburgers, three orders of fries, and three black and white milk shakes," Toad said. "Okay, guys?"

"Fine," B.J. said.

Florence scribbled on her pad and then yelled over to the cook behind the counter. He was a high school kid who worked there on weekends. Sam Sandwich, or whatever the owner's name was, only cooked on weekdays. It was said that he was out on Saturdays hunting down the meat for the rest of the week. There had been a real shortage of opossums in our town lately.

"Joe, three burgers and fries."

I heard him flip the beef patties onto the grill and sink the already cooked fries back into the grease pit to warm up. Florence went behind the counter to manufacture the milk shakes.

"Thanks for the movie," Toad said. He was already bouncing the salt shaker in a napkin, like a little man on a trampoline. Sometimes I even wondered if Toad played games in his sleep.

"Any time," I replied.

"What a bunch of idiots," B.J. said. "Do you believe how they botched that jewelry job? Even we could have done better than that."

"Maybe the perfect crime we plan ought to be a jewel robbery," Toad suggested. "We could work something out with the Louella Jewelry Store or something."

"No good," B.J. said. "Jewelry's dumb. Besides, there's nothing in that store that doesn't dissolve in water."

"I saw a television show last week about an almost perfect murder," Toad said. "But the guy got caught in the end."

"Why?" I asked.

"I forgot."

"Must have been some great show," I said.

"I was doing my math homework at the time. I wasn't really concentrating."

Florence arrived with the food. We jumped at it, scarfing down everything at once.

"Leave a little of the milk shake, Chad. And, B.J., don't eat all your fries. It has to look like we aren't finished yet when we're done."

"Why?"

"You'll see in a few minutes."

We didn't talk much while we worked our way

38

through the food. I was dying to drain my milk shake glass, but I followed Toad's order and kept about an inch at the bottom. B.J. finished most of his fries and then started on mine. Toad left about half of his hamburger uneaten.

"Finished?" Toad asked when we'd slowed down to a medium gobble.

"Yeah, I guess so."

"Stand by," Toad said and pulled a school milk carton out of his pocket. He checked to see whether either Florence or the high school cook were looking our way. They weren't. They were talking with each other over the counter. The high school kid was trying to get a look down the front of her uniform. It looked like he was doing yoga exercises with his neck.

Toad opened the milk carton and pulled a dead cockroach out by a leg. It was a big one, almost an inch long.

"From school," he explained. "I caught it in the storage closet outside the cafeteria. It was resting on a loaf of Wonder bread."

I wasn't surprised. Someday the roaches were going to take over the school. If you got to a dance early, you could see them pack their bags and scatter as the crowds arrived. There was a rumor that someone saw a small herd of them carrying one of the lunchroom cashiers off into the dark recesses of the basement.

Toad lifted the top hamburger roll and flipped the unappetizing insect onto what was left of his hamburger. He put the roll back on top and picked the burger up.

"Here's to you," he said, moving the bun toward his mouth for a bite.

I thought he was actually going to take a chew on it, but he stopped it just a fraction short, looked down crosseyed at the feeler dangling out of the bun and he let out an unholy scream.

"Jesus!" he yelled. "Yuck. I'm going to die."

Florence came strolling over to the table.

"I don't believe it! I just don't believe it," Toad said. "I think I'm going to be sick." He was playing it for all it was worth, a budding Academy Award winner. He even looked a little green around the ears.

"What's the matter, kid?" Florence asked. She didn't miss a chew on her gum. She even snapped it briefly for emphasis.

"Jesus, God," Toad said. "Look what was in my hamburger."

He thrust the roll up toward her and lifted the top of the bun. The roach lay there, feet in the air, lightly coated with grease.

"What kind of a place is this?" Toad shouted.

The high school cook came from behind the counter. The two people who had been sitting up front swiveled in their stools and looked our way.

"The kid got a roach in his hamburger," Florence said. "What do ya think of that."

"Couldn't of happened," the high school kid said. "I cooked them myself. Them patties ain't big enough to hide a roach in. He's probably pulling a fast one."

"Listen," Toad said, "I just may barf right here on the table. This is the most disgusting thing I've ever seen. God, a roach! Maybe it crawled into the roll before you put the hamburger in."

"Is it dead?" Florence asked.

"Yeah, it's dead. I almost bit its goddam head off."

"Pretty ugly," the high school kid said. "You want another burger?"

"Are you kidding me? But I'll tell you one thing. I'm sure not going to pay for this one. Or my friends either."

Someone at the counter was shouting for coffee so the high school kid went back to his spot in front of the grill.

"You don't have to pay for the burger. The rest you pay for."

"Listen, Florence, this is really gross. You're lucky I don't report this to the Board of Health. I mean, there ought to be some kind of law about this."

"Tell you what. You pay for everything but the hamburger and I'll tell the boss about it when he comes in on Monday and you stop by Monday afternoon. The boss'll give you a refund on the rest if he thinks he should. Fair?"

"Hell, Florence. That's not fair. We shouldn't have to pay for any of this garbage."

"You're lucky I don't charge extra for the roach. It's got more meat on it than the hamburger," she said. I think her hand was glued to her hip. I'd never seen her stand any other way.

"I'll shout bloody murder," Toad said. "I'll make up picket signs and march in front of the diner all week." I could tell he was getting desperate.

"Sorry, kid. You owe me for three fries, three shakes, and two burgers."

"I'll report it to the police."

"So report it."

"I'll write a letter to the *Louella Times*."

"So write a letter. Just pay me for the food is all."

"Jesus," Toad said, digging out his wallet. "It just doesn't seem fair. I mean, I get a goddam cockroach in my hamburger and you should give us a ten-dollar gift certificate, not that I'd ever eat in this place again even it was the last food on earth."

He gave Florence the money. She took it, stuffed it into her uniform pocket, and went on back to the counter.

"Well, it was a good try," I said. "I mean, you almost got away with it. Almost perfect. There's nothing wrong with the idea. Florence is just too hard to crack." I was talking too much, but I was trying to make Toad feel better. He's always been a poor loser.

"Shit, you blew it," B.J. said, shaking his head. "And I thought we had a pretty good thing going here."

"It really ticks me off," Toad said. "I was sure it was going to work. That damn Florence."

"Yeah? Well, it didn't. Hell," B.J. said and finished off the rest of my milk shake.

I turned to Toad. "You had a great idea. That's what counts. Listen, B.J., it's the idea, right? So it misfired a little. So what."

"You think it was a good idea?" Toad said. He looked like a basset hound.

"I think we should forget the whole thing," B.J. said.

"It was just for practice, after all," I said. "We're entitled to a few mistakes, aren't we?"

"Not if we're serious."

"Who's serious? I thought it was supposed to be a game," I said.

"I'll do better next time, B.J. Really I will."

42

"You'd better believe it," B.J. said and stood up. Toad and I followed and grabbed our jackets and headed for the door.

Toad turned back toward the counter. "This place is disgusting," he shouted. "Do you know that they have bugs in their food?" The two people at the counter looked briefly at us and then went back to their coffee. It was nothing new to them.

Florence smiled. "See you next week, kids. Thanks for stopping by."

We walked out into the dark.

"Well, at least you got one of the hamburgers for free. That's part of a perfect crime anyway," I said to Toad.

"Think she knew it was my roach?"

"Of course she did. She's not as dumb as you are."

"Hell, B.J. I still think it was a good idea," I said.

B.J. stopped and looked at us for a minute. The wind blew his nylon hood up the back of his head.

"It was all right," he said. "We're still a team."

Toad smiled. "Thanks. Now what about the drink that you're in charge of. I hope you do better than I did."

I felt better too. Arguing makes me feel uncomfortable. Especially when the three of us disagree. It happens all the time and I guess that's natural, but I always feel better when the argument's over and everything's smooth like I like it to be.

"Don't worry, buddy. I will. Follow me. It's time to toast our training."

Toad let out a whoop.

It was snowing much harder by then, blowing in from the west along Lancaster Avenue. There wasn't much traffic on the road, but when a car did pass by, as we were waiting for the light on the corner, the snow swirled up around its tires and flashed through its headlights.

The light turned green and B.J. led the way across the street and away from Lancaster Avenue, up past Episcopal Church and across the street from the school grounds. The fields were filling up with snow. A few lights shone from classroom windows, probably the janitor crew sweeping up the week's accumulation of trash.

We went the two blocks to Windermere Avenue and grabbed a left. B.J. was walking quickly. He knew where he was headed. I turned the collar up on my ski parka to keep the snow from creeping down the back of my neck.

About halfway down the block, we crossed the street to the other side. The houses were hazy in the snow, the huge trees blurred.

"You guys got to be quiet now," B.J. said. I almost laughed. We hadn't said a word in five minutes. "Up here."

We followed B.J. up the driveway of one of the old houses on Windermere. There were lights on in the living room and a light on upstairs. They cast squares of yellow on the white ground. There must have been almost an inch of snow already, it was coming down so fast.

B.J. stopped behind the house in front of the closed doors of the two-car attached garage.

"We have to be careful here," B.J. said. "The kitchen's on the other side of the garage. If someone's in the kitchen, they might hear us. There isn't any light on in there, so I think we'll be all right."

B.J. reached down and eased the garage door up about three feet. It rumbled on its rollers. He paused a minute, waiting, but there was no reaction from inside.

"Come on," he said and stooped down, sliding in underneath. Toad and I ducked down behind him. The air inside the garage was still. It was fine to get away from the swirling snow. There was one car in the garage. The other side was filled with garden tools, bikes, and a lawn mower.

I could see a door at the back of the garage that probably led to the kitchen. Next to the door stood a big, old refrigerator. The three of us crossed the concrete floor and B.J. pulled the refrigerator door open. The light inside lit up and I could see that the shelves were filled with a couple of cases of beer and a few half gallons of wine. There was even one of those little keglets with the spouts.

"What'll it be, gentlemen?" B.J. asked. "It's on the house."

"Jeez, I don't care," Toad said. "Beer?"

"No. Too cold for beer. How about a bottle of wine?"

"Sounds good," I said. "Maybe it'll warm us up."

B.J. reached into the refrigerator and grabbed a bottle of Gallo Hearty Burgundy by its neck and pulled it out. He held it up into the light and then eased the refrigerator door shut. We scurried out of the garage. B.J. slid the garage door down again and we were off with our loot.

We ran back down the driveway to Windermere, turned left, and headed toward the school grounds again.

We stopped at the corner of Louella and Windermere to get our breath. We puffed out clouds of smoke into the cold air. B.J. pulled the bottle out from underneath his jacket and it glinted in the light from the street lamp.

"What did I tell you. On the house, right?"

"How'd you know about that?" I asked.

"My brother told me. He used to swipe beer all the time last summer before he went off to school. It was his going away present to me, but he warned me never to take too much so that they'd catch on. No sense ruining a good thing. They keep so much in that spare ice box that they never seem to miss a six pack here or there. It's the first time I've tried it though."

"Next time you talk to your brother, give him my thanks," Toad said. "I can use something to warm me up right about now."

"Not here," B.J. said. He shoved the bottle back under his parka and we crossed the street and went through the iron gate into the school grounds. Pieces of disused playground equipment loomed up out of the snow, relics from before the junior high annexed the elementary school. The football field was a sea of white.

"Where are we going to drink this stuff?" I asked. "I don't much feel like staying out in the cold."

"Can't go to my place. My parents are home," Toad said.

"Mine too."

"We'll be all right if we can find somewhere out of this wind," B.J. said. "How about the handball courts?"

We headed across the field to the back of the old elementary school building. The three handball courts, three-sided cubes built into the back of the gym wall, lay ahead of us in the snow.

We reached them and entered the one closest to

the building. B.J. was right. As soon as we got between the walls, the wind died out and it seemed much warmer.

We went to the far corner and brushed the snow off the ground as best as we could. We sat down, huddling together for warmth. B.J. pulled the bottle back out and screwed off the lid. He took a long swig, exhaled a cloud of breath, and passed it to Toad. Toad grabbed a swallow and gave the bottle to me. I put the bottle to my lips and lifted. I let the cold wine flow down my throat. I took another long swallow and then passed it back to B.J.

We leaned against the handball wall, three in a row, wrapped in our coats, pulled up tight under our chins and over our ears.

The wine turned warm in my stomach and left a strong burning taste in the back of my mouth. It was good stuff.

"Congratulations," B.J. said. "We all pass Training Test Number Two."

"I didn't," Toad said. "I only got us one of the hamburgers for free."

"One's enough. It'll do."

"You didn't think so before," I said.

"Well, I do now."

B.J. took another swig and the bottle of wine started around the circle again.

"It hits the spot," Toad said. "I don't feel so cold anymore."

"We must look like a bunch of loonies, sitting out here in the snow swilling wine," I said.

"Want to go home?" B.J. asked.

"No way," I said and drained some more of the wine. Toad was right. It did seem warmer. I felt amazingly comfortable and at ease sitting there in the handball court in the darkness.

"It's been fun," Toad said. "The whole thing. I can still see Mr. Patterson's nose crinkling up in class like he'd just stepped in a pile of dog crap."

"It's not over yet," B.J. said. "I've thought up one more test before we settle down to plan our perfect crime."

"Yeah? What is it?" I asked.

"On Monday, after school, each of us picks somebody to follow. You have to trail the person without being seen, all the way to the home or until they get in a car or something. Without being seen. After all, we can't be big-time crooks unless we have stealth and the ability to shadow someone." B.J. laughed softly in the dark.

"And you have to bring some proof back that you followed them," I suggested.

"Good. Something concrete, so we know each of us did the job right."

"Pass me the wine, will you?" Toad said.

B.J. gave him the bottle. It was about half empty by then and I think we were feeling the effects. At least I was. I felt light headed and the cold didn't bother me at all anymore.

"If we can each get away with that, then we know we've got the makings of first-class criminals. Planning the perfect crime should be a cinch."

Toad passed the bottle back to me and I took another long pull on it. The edge of the bottle mouth wasn't cold anymore either.

"But we still don't know what we're going to be planning," I said.

"Who cares?" Toad said. "I mean it. I haven't

had so much fun since I don't know when. We'll cross that bridge when we get to it."

"We should do stuff like this more often," B.J. said. "What every young American needs is a purpose in life. Some direction. A goal. Like Patterson says, a mind doesn't know its potentials until it's stretched to the limits." He lifted the bottle into the air in a toast.

"Screw Patterson," Toad said. "We're having too good a time to think about him."

"Have you read the *Paradise Lost* assignment for Monday yet?" I asked.

"Are you kidding me?"

"No. I read it before dinner tonight. It's not bad stuff. Satan gets heaved out of heaven and goes sailing down to hell. It's pretty interesting if you can get through all the fancy words."

When night
Darkens the streets, then wander forth the sons
Of Belial, flown with insolence and wine.

"Remind me about it Monday morning, will you?" B.J. said. "I don't want to think about homework on Friday night, that's for sure. Particularly one like this. I don't get a chance to get shitfaced with my friends every day of the week."

The bottle was almost finished.

I tilted my head back and looked up. The world was white. The handball court was white; the sky was white; and the snow swirled in spirals just beyond us where the wind started blowing. The wine was burning in my stomach and along the back of my throat and I was comfortable. Snow flakes gathered on my eyelashes. I looked at Toad and B.J.

and their heads were white with the snow too. Everything was white. I felt like I had been anesthetized and wrapped in white gauze. I could just lie back and be buried in snow. Disappear in a blanket of purity. The three of us, covered over in a mound of snow, perfectly still, perfectly cold, perfectly preserved. And I didn't care a bit. Toad laughed quietly next to me.

"Shit, this is really something, huh?" He passed me the bottle and I drained it. Then I threw the bottle at the back wall and it shattered. The shards of glass fell in slow motion with the flakes of snow and were buried in whiteness.

We all laughed.

It had been a perfect night.

Almost.

We sat there awhile, slumped against the handball court walls, not saying anything. Just sort of soaking up the quiet. Then suddenly Toad jumped up and dashed out into the open field. He got about five feet away and created a Gallo ice cone all over the snow. It was like the evening in review as he spilled his guts out onto the snow. Wine and French fries steaming on the snow. It wasn't exactly appetizing and I felt my own stomach do a flip or two, but the burning lump stopped somewhere in the back of my throat.

Even the best moments never last.

Toad stood there making retching sounds and holding his head in his hands. The wind whipped the snow up around him, and I noticed the cold again and began shivering.

"Jesus Christ," B.J. said. "You've got all the class of a cockroach."

Toad just shook his head and groaned.

"I'll see you guys on Monday," B.J. said and walked off across the open school field, eventually disappearing into the sheets of snow.

I went over to Toad. He was still breathing heavily.

"You okay?"

"Yeah. Sure."

"Let's go," I said and we walked as far as Upland Way together before I split off into the storm alone. I couldn't tell which was swirling more, the snow or my head.

I never did get sick. I made it home and up to bed without my parents noticing my condition. But all day Saturday I sure knew my stomach was still pissed off at me.

CHAPTER 3

We met in the halls by our lockers at three on Monday and went over the rules one last time.

The third training test wasn't going to be as easy as it sounded.

B.J. went through the deal: "You pick somebody and follow them. You can't get spotted or you've blown it. And you have to bring something back that proves you followed them as long as you could. That's the important part."

"It can be anybody, right?" Toad asked.

"It doesn't matter who it is, just as long as you do it right this time."

"Bring the proof with you tomorrow. We can compare notes at lunch," I suggested.

"And don't blow it, huh?" B.J. said. "This is the one that tells us whether it's worth going any further with this crime stuff."

I slammed the locker door and got into my jacket. The three of us went down the front steps to the door.

"Good luck, you guys. We're on our own."

We went out into the cold air. The snow had stopped on Saturday. There must have been almost half a foot of it. It would have been a for-sure snow day at school if it hadn't been a weekend. By Sunday the roads were clear and dry and by now patches of gray winter grass were beginning to show through again.

"See you," Toad said and started off toward the bus loop. He was almost running. I figured he already knew who he was going to trail. B.J. gave me a wave and started up toward the center of Louella, a block away. He ambled along, tossing a snow ball in his hand, trying to look casual, but by the way he gave everyone on the sidewalk the once over, I knew he was on the lookout for a possible victim to follow.

I had no idea in mind at all. I thought I'd just wait around until someone interesting came along and then follow along right behind.

A few students came out of the school doors, but I cancelled them out. Who wants to follow another kid? Besides, I knew most everybody, where they lived and all, so there wasn't any challenge there. I wanted to really prove my skill.

I walked down the sidewalk and stood in front of the firehouse. I watched the people go in and out of the post office across the street. I thought that maybe some likely candidate would show up sooner or later. I crossed off a housewifely type with a baby in a stroller and businessman rushing toward the bank on the corner. I knew I couldn't put off my decision too long though. It was three-thirty already and I was expected home for dinner before five-thirty. I had no idea how long trailing somebody was likely to take.

Then Mr. Patterson walked by.

"Hello, Chad," he said.

"Hi, Mr. Patterson."

"I liked your comment about Satan suffering from too much pride in class today. You seem to know what you read."

"Thanks. I'm kind of enjoying *Paradise Lost*. I really am."

"You may be alone in that category, but I'm glad to hear it. Keep up the good work. Maybe you can wipe out that failure before the end of the semester," he said.

"I hope so."

"I was sorry I had to fail you yesterday. I just want you to understand that it's my policy. It was nothing personal against you as a student. You usually do very fine work."

"Thank you," I said.

"You don't think I was fair, do you?"

I shrugged. What was I going to say?

"Would you like me to move your seat so you're not next to B.J.?"

"No, sir. I won't let it happen again."

"I hope not. I'd have to fail you again."

"I know."

"Well, see you tomorrow," Mr. Patterson said and walked on past me, past the firehouse, and past the teachers' parking lot.

As I watched him walking away, I realized how little I knew about him. About any of my teachers, to be exact. Somehow you don't expect that they actually live anywhere and have lives of their own. I remember in third grade, my teacher had gotten to school early on a Monday morning and hid in the closet. When we had all arrived and gotten to our seats, she walked out of the closet as if nothing was out of the ordinary. And none of us were surprised.

It didn't seem strange to us at all that maybe she lived in there.

I'd been in Mr. Patterson's class a whole year and he was a complete mystery. I fell into step about ten yards behind him.

He continued up to the main corner of Louella and waited for the walk light. I hung back, looking at the portraits in a photographer's window. I had seen them a million times before. They'd been in the window for months. The walk light flashed and Mr. Patterson started across. I had to move quickly to catch the same light, so I picked up speed and started across just as the DON'T WALK sign started blinking. Mr. Patterson turned right and went into the Louella Book and Record Shoppe.

I stood on the corner feeling stupid. I didn't want to go into the store after him and I didn't much want to stand on the corner like an idiot until he came out. So I walked on past the book store and sat down on the stone wall in front of the Presbyterian Church, about twenty yards from the store.

It was a popular wall. Some of the kids from the high school had staked it out and could always be found loitering there on Saturdays. Today there wasn't anyone but me. It was a good place. I could see the entrance to the book store and I didn't look very conspicuous. As I said, there were always kids sitting on the wall.

I must have sat there for almost a half hour waiting for Mr. Patterson to reappear. It seemed much longer. A couple of girls from my section walked by and stopped to talk for a few minutes, but it didn't really make the time go much faster. My bottom just got colder and wetter as the snow melted beneath me. I kept my hands in my pockets to keep my fingers from falling off.

Finally, out of the corner of my eye, I saw Mr. Patterson leave the book store. He had a package under his arm. I was hoping he wouldn't turn my way. Seeing each other again would only bring attention to myself and I sure didn't want that.

He headed back for the main corner, but instead of crossing the intersection again, he turned right and disappeared from view.

I jumped off the wall and ran to the corner. I looked around the edge of the building and saw him about twenty yards ahead of me, walking up North Louella Avenue. I turned the corner too and kept going at a steady pace behind him.

He paused to look in the candy store window and then crossed North Louella and went into Rexall's. I stayed on my side of the street, looking in the candy store window myself. I saw in the reflection when he left Rexall's and then popped into the state liquor store. In a few minutes he came out of there with another bag under his arm.

I waited where I was, watching him cross back to my side of the street and continue north. When his back was to me and he was walking at a fast pace, I left the candy store behind and followed after him.

At the end of the block was the train station, the town's stop on the Paoli Local which runs the commuters to and from Philadelphia each day. It's a rickety old station, with Victorian curlicues and faded paint. I could see Mr. Patterson go up to the platform and then down the stairs that led to the tunnel under the tracks. I ran to the top of the steps and, when I couldn't hear his footsteps echoing in the tunnel any longer, went down the stairs after him.

When I reached the tunnel, I heard him walking up the steps on the other side, onto the westbound train platform. I walked through the tunnel. It always smelled a little bit like old toilets, and the walls were covered with scrawls and graffiti. My favorite one, written in green paint, was "It's hell to be lost in your bathing suit." It had been there for as long as I could remember and I always wondered who had written it.

At the end of the tunnel, I looked up the stairs to the platform and I could see Mr. Patterson sitting on one of the benches. He had pulled a paperback from his bag and was reading it.

I figured I was safe enough where I was, in the darkness of the tunnel, and as long as he was reading, there wasn't any chance he would spot me.

I remained where I was until he made his next move. The shadowing had taken on real excitement. I felt like I used to when I was a little kid and we played hide and go seek on summer nights with flashlights. It was fun and a challenge. I had thought it might end up being a pain, but B.J. was right. It was good practice and mental exercise.

I heard the roar of an incoming train and looked up the stairwell. Mr. Patterson was standing, putting the book back in the bag. He stepped out of my line of vision as he moved toward the tracks.

The train screeched as it braked and I started up the steps. I wanted to make sure I caught the last car before it pulled out of the station.

It was a dinky little middle-of-the-day train that Penn Central runs during off hours. It was only three cars long. I grabbed the handle of the last car and swung myself aboard. I hoped that Mr. Patterson had gotten on one of the forward cars. If he saw me I was screwed. I didn't have any excuse for taking the train and he would be sure to ask. I could always say I was going to a dentist appointment.

The car was half empty. I moved forward and looked through the window into the car ahead. Mr. Patterson was sitting about halfway up, facing front. I recognized the back of his head and his brown suede coat.

I stood there at the window letting my weight bounce back and forth with the jogging of the train.

"Ticket, please."

I turned and the conductor was behind me. I pulled out my wallet. I didn't know how far Mr. Patterson was riding.

"Roud trip to Paoli," I said and gave him the money.

Paoli was the end of the line, six stops away. He couldn't be going any further than that.

The conductor took my money and punched away at the ticket. He handed me the return slip. Then he pushed his way through the connecting door and began taking tickets in the next car.

I ended up wasting most of the fare because the train pulled up at the next stop, Stratford, and Mr. Patterson stood up. He turned my way and I ducked down, sliding into the seat closest to the door. I ran back to the other end of the car and jumped off at the last minute.

I was just in time to see Mr. Patterson going down the steps from the station toward Old Eagle School Road. I waited at the top until he turned in under the train bridge and then I followed. By the time I got to the bottom and peeked around the corner, I saw Mr. Patterson cross the road and head up the driveway to the Stratford Station Apartments.

The Stratford Station Apartments are the two-and-a-half-story garden apartment types, arranged in a cluster of about ten separate buildings. Mr. Patterson went off the shoveled sidewalk onto a well-trodden path in the snow. He cut across the open area behind one of the buildings and went in the back door.

Okay. I had done it, followed him all the way to his home without being caught. Now I had to find something to prove it. I raced around to the front of the building and dashed up the short flight of steps. I pushed open the door to Building H, Mr. Patterson's, and stood inside a small hallway where one short set of stairs led up to the second floor and another set led down to the basement level.

In the hallway was a table with the day's mail spread out in neat piles, one for each apartment. I glanced over the piles quickly and found one letter with Mr. Patterson's name on it. Without even really thinking, I stuffed it into my parka pocket. I had my proof.

I also noticed a *Playboy* magazine in its neat brown wrapper lying on the table. It wasn't addressed to Mr. Patterson, but I couldn't resist. I took it too and ran out through the front door and back up the drive toward the train station.

While I was waiting for the train, I checked out the magazine. The Playmate of the Month was a real winner. She hung out all over the staples. I looked through the second half for the jokes and when I saw an eastbound train coming, I stuffed the *Playboy* in my looseleaf notebook. I climbed aboard when the train stopped at the platform.

What with the five-minute train ride back to Louella and the ten-minute walk home from the station, I got in the front door before five. The lights of the house glowed orange in the blue of the evening as I walked up the driveway. I could see that my little sister had been making angels in the snow all over the lawn. It made me mad. The snow looked dumpy and used. I always like it better when our lawn stretched untouched down to the street.

I hung my coat in the front hall closet. Good smells were coming from the kitchen.

"Hi, it's me," I yelled.

"Glad you're home," Mom shouted. "Have a good day?" Her voice carried with the odors from the kitchen.

"Fine," I yelled back. "I'll be down in a minute."

I ran up the stairs two at a time and hurried down the hall to my bedroom. I had taken the letter from my coat pocket and when I reached my room, I looked at it again.

The address was: Mr. James Patterson, 410 Stratford Avenue, Apartment 1-C, Stratford, Pa. I flipped the envelope over. There was a return address: Lt. H. Templeton, US Navy, Missouri, Med. Fleet, Marseilles, France. There were French stamps and Par Avion stickers all over the front of the letter. I put it in the middle of the English section of my notebook, to show to Toad and B.J. the next day at lunch.

I took the *Playboy* and stuffed it under the mattress along with a small book of dirty comics I'd found in one of the trash cans at school the month before. I shoved them both further under so my mother wouldn't discover them. I'd have to find another place before spring when she turned the mattress during her annual super-clean. Even if she did find them, I don't suspect she'd say anything about them to me. My mother's the kind of person who would just put them back where they were and never let on.

I went back downstairs and wandered out to the kitchen.

"Hi," I said. Mom was at the counter near the refrigerator ripping lettuce up for a salad.

"Hi."

I lifted the lid of the cookie jar and took out about five Oreos. No matter whatever happened, there were always Oreos in the cookie jar. I suspect the world could come to an end, and the Oreos would continue to appear like magic inside that jar.

"Don't eat too many. We'll be having dinner soon. Your dad's got a directors' meeting at eight."

"Is he home yet?" I asked.

"No. Should be soon."

"Where's Janey?"

Over at the Allans'. She and Stephanie were playing this afternoon over here. But when Janey found out we were having meatloaf for dinner, they went across the street to see what Stephanie was having. Pot roast, so the Allans won out."

"Or lost. Serves the Allans right. We had to put up with Stephie the night before last."

"It must be nice to have a choice of two menus every night."

"Don't the Allans ever get sick of her? Janey's such a pain."

"And you're such a gem to have around?"

"I'm intelligent, brave, honest, and forthright," I said. "So who could get tired of me?"

"I could. Any homework?"

"Yeah. English as usual and a little math."

"Then why don't you get at it. I'll call you when dinner's ready."

"Okay, I'll get it over with," I said, grabbing a few more cookies. I went back upstairs to my room. I sat down at my desk and pulled out the English anthology and began reading about Satan's plans for the Garden of Eden in *Paradise Lost*.

I'd only read a few lines when I noticed the corner of the letter sticking out from inside my notebook. I looked away, trying to concentrate on the Milton, but I couldn't do it. My eyes kept drifting back to the letter.

Finally, I pulled it out again and turned it over in my hands a few times. It was starting to bother me. Maybe it was something important, and for the first time it occurred to me that what I had done was illegal. I mean, tampering with the mails was some kind of federal offense or something.

First I thought that maybe I should just rip it up into little pieces and flush it down the john. Then I thought that maybe I should sneak it back to Mr. Patterson's apartment the next day. But I always came back to the conclusion that if I didn't bring the letter to show to B.J. and Toad then I wouldn't have any proof that I'd trailed Mr. Patterson at all. And it was too good a thing to throw away. Hell, I knew I had the best proof of either of them. There was no way they could top shadowing Mr. Patterson. For some dumb reason, it was just too important. I knew if I didn't bring it, B.J. would end up cutting right through me the way he does to Toad all the time. I couldn't let that happen, could I? We were all in this together and I wanted them to be impressed.

As it turned out, I couldn't have done a dumber thing. I only wish I could have known it then. But I didn't, so I decided to be pleased with myself and figured I'd come out on top.

I did tuck the letter back into the notebook, completely out of sight, and tried to get back to my reading. It wasn't easy.

We didn't get a chance to talk about our Training Test Number Three until lunch. I had sat impatiently through Mr. Patterson's melodramatic reading of Satan's speeches in English, wanting to know the whole time how Toad and B.J. had made out in their shadowing the day before. I had the letter to Mr. Patterson safely tucked in my notebook, proof positive that I had been able to accomplish the job. I'd stopped arguing with myself and couldn't wait until B.J. and Toad saw it.

We settled in at a corner table in the cafeteria and put our heads together. The noise seemed to diminish in the background.

"I pulled it off," Toad said, munching on what looked like a peanut butter and dill pickle sandwich. "And I learned a thing or two while I was at it."

"Who'd you follow?" I asked, spooning up runny baked beans from my plate. The school served hot dogs and baked beans every Tuesday, no matter what.

"Roxanne Spiese. I figured she'd never spot me. People are always following her."

"Jesus, Roxanne Spiese! Wouldn't you know," B.J. said, leaning on the table, working his way through an ice cream sandwich. "And she didn't know you were trailing her?"

63

"Nope."

"And you followed her all the way home?"

"Yep. But it took me until almost six o'clock. She took a very interesting detour first." Toad slumped back in his chair with a dirty-old-man look plastered all over his face.

"Tell us," I said. "I can't stand the suspense."

"Well, I picked her up outside the student commons."

"That'll be the day," B.J. laughed.

"Not picked up, picked up. You know. I stood out by the bus loop to see where she was headed. I froze my tail off while she hung around inside. Finally, this kid shows up and she goes running like crazy up to meet him. Some tall, dark-haired kid, hair all slicked back, trying to look like a tough guy. Anyway, the two of them leave the commons and start walking up South Louella. She carried his book and that left his hands free to wander all over her backside."

"Sounds like a disgusting display of public affection," B.J. said.

"And how. Disgusting all right. I would have given anything to have been that pair of hands."

"So where'd they go?"

"Well, very interesting. I didn't know who the guy was, although I think I remember seeing him around. Roxanne doesn't mess around with us nice guys, I guess."

"I told you she knows where the action is."

"They turned up West Avenue and walked a few blocks. I stayed pretty far behind. They weren't in any hurry, and I thought if I got any closer, Roxanne might catch on. The guy wouldn't have cared. He was too busy with other things."

"Yeah?"

"They crossed over Conestoga Road and then went into a little brick ranch-house type place a block or so beyond. It was his house. He had the key to the front door, anyway."

"So was that it?" B.J. asked. "That's as far as you trailed her?" He gave a short snort.

"Hell, that wasn't the end of it at all. I hung around, a few houses down, figuring I had better wait and follow Roxanne all the way home to her own house. That was the deal, wasn't it?"

"You better believe it." B.J. was on his second ice cream sandwich.

"Well, it got pretty cold just standing there. I didn't have any idea how long she was going to be in there. Maybe she was going to spend the night, for all I knew."

"Sounds like Roxanne."

"After a half hour or so, I thought I could creep up to the house and look in the window and see whether I could tell if she was going to be there much longer. Deal or no deal, I was verging on pneumonia. I thought that even you guys would admit that a live criminal is better than a dead one. I snuck up the next-door driveway and crossed over through some pine trees and peeked in the window. I couldn't believe it."

"What? What?" I asked. I pictured Toad with his nose perched on the windowsill like a bald little bird.

"They were on the couch together, going to town. I mean really going at it. There were two beer bottles on the coffee table and a few cigarette butts in the ash tray."

"Did they have their clothes off?" B.J. asked.

"Oh, no. But they were lying on the couch going crazy. I tell you, Roxanne is some hot number all right. You knew what you were talking about, B.J. Her hands were all over him. And he wasn't doing so badly, either. Well, I hung around the window for a little bit. It was really something to see, but I was fogging the glass up and I didn't want to press my luck. I ran back into the pine trees. And it was a good thing I did because a few minutes later, a car pulls into the driveway of the guy's house and a lady gets out. His mother, I guess. She goes up to the front door and lets herself in. A little bit later, Roxanne goes out the front door and says in this real loud voice, so the mother will hear her, 'Thanks for the help on the homework, Vinnie. See you tomorrow.' Then she gives her ass a little wiggle and goes on out to the street.

"I gave her a half a block lead and then I followed her the rest of the way home. She lives over in North Louella on Chestnut Lane."

"Good man, Toad. You pass."

"Thanks, but I'll probably still get pneumonia anyway," Toad said.

"Where's your proof?" I asked. I didn't want them to forget about the proof since I had mine ready and waiting.

"Oh, yeah," Toad said. He pulled a metal number out of his shirt pocket. It was a small 2, black on gold with a sticky backing.

"This is one of the numbers off the house sign on a light pole by their front sidewalk. 259 Chestnut Lane. I peeled it off the sign and brought it along."

"That'll do just fine," B.J. said.

"Think maybe Roxanne will go out with me if I ask her to the dance next week?" Toad asked.

"Are you kidding?" B.J. said and laughed.

"I was just sort of wondering. That guy Vinnie really has it made."

"How about you, B.J.? How'd your tailing go?" I asked.

"Fine. I learned a thing or two myself."

"Who was it?"

"I don't even know her name. Some old lady. I went up to the Acme and started strolling around the aisles, thinking I'd pick up someone who was shopping. I spotted this old lady. She must have been a hundred and ten. I decided to trail her. She seemed like an easy mark, if you know what I mean. She was pushing one of those grocery carts around. Not that kind that you get at the store, but the kind that little old ladies bring with them. Once I saw that, I guessed that she must walk to the grocery store and back, so I'd be able to follow her all the way home. If I chose somebody that drove, I'd end up losing them.

"I got a cart for myself, so I didn't look like I was doing anything but shopping and began following her up and down the aisles. She was really incredible."

"Why?" I asked.

"Because she was a shoplifter. No kidding. She was a real pro. She had this big winter coat on with about fifty pockets on the inside she must have sewed into the lining. Anything big she dropped into her cart, but anything small, she stuffed inside her coat."

"Seriously?"

"Seriously. She'd give a quick check around to see if anyone was watching and then, plunk, inside

67

the coat it would go. She must have gained fifty pounds while I watched. Cat food, tuna fish, candy bars, a jar of jam, even a package of cream cheese. She had about five bucks worth of stuff in her cart and about twenty bucks under her coat. She was fast too. It wasn't her first time ripping off the Acme. You could tell. She had everything down to a science. The hand was faster than the eye. When she was all done, she wheeled her cart up to the checkout counter. All of a sudden she changed. Instead of being quick and sharp, she started acting dumb and doddery. She managed to get the stuff out of the cart onto the counter and the girl checked her through without even looking at her. Seven dollars and fifty-three cents worth. She paid the girl and the girl rang the money up and put the stuff into the lady's push-cart.

"I ditched the cart I'd been pushing and then I followed the old lady out of the store. She was a smooth number, I'll tell you. She went out through the doors and just maneuvered the cart along as if nothing was wrong. When she got to the corner of the building, she went around the edge and behind a Salvation Army drop-off bin, out of sight from the parking lot. I watched her unload her coat and put the stuff into the cart along with the things she had paid for. It was like clowns coming out of a Volkswagen in the circus, she had so many things stuffed under the coat. The cart was only half full when she left the store; now it was almost spilling over.

"Then she continued on down the street. I trailed her. I still needed to follow her home and get proof at the same time. So about a block later, I caught up with her and asked if I could push the cart for her. She said sure and I took over pushing the hot groceries the rest of the way to her house."

"How far?"

"Just another block or two. She lived on the ground floor of one of those old, run-down converted houses on Runnymede. All the way along, she kept talking about how expensive things were getting and how she had trouble making ends meet on her Social Security check. No wonder she rips stuff off from the Acme."

"So what proof did you bring?" Toad asked.

"Right here," B.J. said and he pulled a long slip of paper out of his pocket. He passed it over to me. It was the shopping total, a long list of figures with a sum of seven dollars and fifty-three cents.

"I pulled it out of her grocery bag when I was carrying it up the porch for her."

"Maybe we should let her in on our plans," Toad said. "Sounds like she could teach us plenty."

"You know, Toad, I guess about anyone could. I mean, it would take us a lot longer to find a totally honest person than to plan the perfect crime."

"I don't know, B.J.," I said. "There are a lot of honest people around. We're pretty honest, after all."

B.J. laughed. "Us honest?"

"Don't believe it, Chad. If you found a wallet with fifty bucks in it, would you turn it over to the cops?" Toad asked.

"Probably," I said. "Especially if there were some identification inside."

"And if there weren't?" B.J. said.

"I don't know. I guess so."

"Then I tell you, Chad, there are two kinds of

people. People who aren't honest, and fools. Guess which one you are? Anyway, who did you shadow?"

"You'll never guess. It was really a kick. I enjoyed the whole thing. It was Mr. Patterson."

"Are you kidding? You followed Mr. Patterson?" Toad said. "And he didn't spot you?"

"Not once. I saw him right outside school. He didn't go into the teachers' parking lot, so I thought that maybe he didn't drive. You know, that I could trail him all the way to where he lives like we agreed."

"Did you?" B.J. asked. He leaned across the table at me. "I'd love to know where that bastard lives. We could send him a bomb special delivery."

"I did. Sure. He browsed in the book store for a while and then bought himself a bottle of booze and then took the train to Stratford. I stayed with him the whole time. We should have a petty-cash fund though. I spent money on that train ride!"

"Tough. So where's he live?" B.J. asked.

"The Stratford Station Apartments."

"It figures. I can't see him in a dump. He probably even makes his bed every morning before school. And does the breakfast dishes too."

"I followed him until he went into one of the back entrances. Then I ran around to the front of the building to get the proof for you guys."

"What did you get?"

"His mail."

"His mail?"

"Yep. There aren't any mailboxes. Just a table in the front hall."

"And you took something?"

"A letter. And guess what?"

"What?"

"A *Playboy* magazine."

"You're kidding," B.J. said. "Patterson reads *Playboy?*"

"No. It was addressed to someone else."

"I wouldn't put it past him though."

"Did you bring it?" Toad asked. "Do you have it here?"

"No, I left it at home."

"Under your mattress, no doubt," B.J. said.

"Correct."

"God, you're original."

"Why didn't you bring it?" Toad asked again.

"Because it was too big to fit in my notebook. And someone ought to put you out of your misery, you horny bastard."

Toad shrugged and finished up his sandwich.

"But I did bring the letter for proof." I'd gone to so much trouble and worried about it so much, I couldn't just let it go by. I pulled it out of my notebook and tossed it on the table, trying to act casual and easy about it as if I liberated mailboxes all the time.

"How about that. Somebody actually writes to Patterson. It's probably a hate note or something. I have trouble believing that there's anyone in the world besides those idiot girls in class who would take the time and money to mail him anything. Let's see it," B.J. said and picked it off the table. It was already sticky on the back from a drying pool of orangeade.

"Mr. James Patterson, 410 Stratford Avenue, Apartment 1-C, Stratford, Pa.," read B.J. "And look at the stamps, will you? It's from France, for Christ's sake."

"Maybe it's from Brigitte Bardot," Toad said.

B.J. turned the letter over and read the return address out loud.

"Sounds like someone in the Navy," he said.

"How's that for proof?" I asked. I guess I was looking for praise.

"First class. You pass."

"Pass? I should get an A."

"Okay. You get an A. Enough already. If we're lucky it's a draft notice."

"Open it," Toad said. "Let's see."

B.J. started to tear at the thin, blue air-mail envelope.

"Hey, wait up a sec, B.J. Maybe we shouldn't read it."

"Jesus what do you think we should do with it?"

"I don't know," I said. "Maybe it's personal."

"Why do you think we're going to open it? Listen, you're the guy that stole it. What are you bitching about. You're not thinking of trying to sneak it back, are you? That's the dumbest thing I've ever heard."

"Wouldn't it be something if you got caught putting it back," Toad said and laughed.

"He can't exactly miss it if he never knew it came," B.J. said.

"I guess so," I said. And I did figure they made sense. Besides I was curious too. I really did want to find out what was in the letter. It's kind of like when someone says they know a great joke but they'd better not tell it to you. It just makes you want to hear it more. Well, the letter was kind of like that. The longer it sat there on the table, the more I wanted it to be opened.

B.J. finished tearing the envelope and pulled the sheets of blue onion-skin paper out.

"Ahem," B.J. cleared his throat. "Gentlemen, the news from abroad."

"Or the news from a broad," I said and Toad laughed again. It made me realize I was being dumb to worry. It was good to hear the laughter.

This was the letter:

Dear Jim,

I was pleased to get your letter, particularly after the months of silence. The best news was the fact that you enjoy teaching so much. It sounds like you've finally found your niche in life. I hope you stay with it and that the rest of your first year goes as smoothly as the first half seems to have. I could tell from your descriptions of the school and your students that your sense of humor is back in full swing. You had me laughing out loud all the way through.

I shared your letter with Steve and Bob. I hope you don't mind, but we all miss you and they were as anxious for news as I was.

It's a shame that whole mess had to happen or you'd be with us still. Now that the training is finally finished and we're lounging around in the Mediterranean sun, things couldn't be easier. Every time we head into Marseilles on leave, I think about you and really do wish you were here. I took a drive last weekend up to Arles to see Van Gogh country and you would have been as overwhelmed as I was. I think you'd like the Navy life now that the basics are over.

At least we've left Conover behind, both of us. The officers on our ship are fine. I've had no complaints since I've been on board. The Navy must save bastards like Conover for basic training. Ever since things went sour for you in Norfolk, I still have trouble believing the way he treated you. I never told you this, but after your breakdown, Bob and I went to Conover to ask him to lay off and the S.O.B. just laughed. It was the closest I have ever come to hitting someone, so I can sympathize with how you must have felt. I can't imagine why he put you through such hell, except that he's the kind of sadist who always needs a victim to cover up his own inadequacies. If it makes you feel any better, I don't think any of us could have stood up under that kind of pressure and persecution.

At least you have your honorable discharge, even though Conover tried to block it. He was furious when he was overruled.

But now you've found something that makes you happy and that's all that's really important. Your Navy experience is past and you're free from its harm.

Please stay in touch. I don't think I'll be in the States again until sometime next year. I'll let you know. Maybe we can get together if we mutually promise *not* to talk over old times. In the meantime, continue to enjoy your teaching and if you ever run into Conover, now that you are an official, full-fledged civilian, take a punch at him again. This time for me, please.

Let us hear from you soon—

Sincerely,
Harry

B.J. put the letter back down on the lunch table and gave a soft whistle through his teeth. "Jesus, what do you know," he said. "We should have suspected all along."

"What?" I asked.

"Patterson's a psycho! Do you believe it, an honest to goodness looney is teaching us English."

"Aw, that's not true," I said, trying to toss it off. "I mean, how can you tell from the letter?" I don't know why I wanted to deny it.

"The hell you can't. It says it right here in black and white. Patterson went bananas during training and flipped his marbles. He even struck his commanding officer! It says all that, doesn't it?"

"I still don't know, B.J."

"Come on, Chad. What, do you have your head wedged or something? It says that, doesn't it, Toad? Huh, doesn't it?" B.J. had that edge in his voice he gets sometimes, so I already knew what Toad was going to say.

"It does sound like it, Chad. It really does," Toad said. "It says he had a breakdown."

"Well, maybe it does. We shouldn't have read the letter. I feel kind of funny about taking it now. I didn't know it was going to be so personal."

"Hell, it was a good thing you did, Chad. We may be the only people who know we've got a teacher who's crazy."

"Jeez, don't you think the principal knows?" Toad asked.

"Of course not. He wouldn't be here if the principal knew. It says right here that he had an honorable discharge. When you apply for a job, you're not about to volunteer the information that you have bats in your belfry and flipped your lid in the Navy.

I mean, nobody would hire you, would they? I sure wouldn't. Jesus, an A-one, certified schizo molding the minds of Louella's youth." B.J. slammed his fist down on the table and laughed out loud. "How about that, huh! Doesn't that really get to you?"

"He seems all right most of the time. I wouldn't have guessed," Toad said.

"That's because you've got the sensitivity of an earthworm. But it just goes to show you. No wonder he's so rotten to us all the time. I must admit, I'm not surprised. I really kind of guessed all along."

"So what are we going to do?" Toad asked. He was excited. B.J.'s hyperness was rubbing off. It always did.

"Nothing. Give me the letter," I said.

"What for?"

"To throw it away."

"Throw it away? You're out of your mind," B.J. said. "Throw away a piece of evidence like this? Not on your life. I think we've just found the answer to our plan for the perfect crime."

"How so?" Toad asked.

"Blackmail!" Give Patterson some of his own medicine. Pay him back for all the shit he's handed out so far this year. Make him sweat a little, just like he makes us sweat every time we walk into his room. See who's got the power now."

"Fantastic," Toad said. "What a fantastic idea."

"You can bet that Patterson would just as soon not have the school board know about his little skeleton in the closet. I think maybe it's about time he has to squirm a little too."

"He can't know it's us. We've got to be careful," Toad said.

"Of course we do. We'll do the whole thing anonymously," B.J. said.

"Do you think that's fair?" I said. I was feeling responsible since it was me that had found the letter, although Lord knows Mr. Patterson deserved all we could dish out. Policy or not, I was still kind of pissed about the quiz the other day. I felt kind of torn. I mean, I suppose I was sorry that I'd ever taken the letter, but now that the whole thing was out in the open, there wasn't a lot I could do about it, was there?

"Of course it isn't fair. But neither is he," B.J. said. "Listen, Chad, if fairness had anything to do with it, he wouldn't have given you an F on that test last week." B.J. always knew the right thing to say. "Or made Steve Sorrell stand leaning against the wall with his hands out for an hour for passing a note. Or, Jesus, remember when he kept Jim a half hour after school for being five minutes late to class and made him miss the basketball game. It was the only one we've lost so far this year, thanks to Patterson. Fairness doesn't have anything to do with what Patterson does. All he cares about is power."

I still wasn't sure I went for the idea. "I thought we were just going to plan a crime, not go through with it. Even you said that, B.J."

"Yah, but that was before we came up with something so perfect. I think you're scared."

"Besides, it's not a crime," Toad chimed in. "It's poetic justice. It only seems right that Mr. Patterson gets a little of his own crap in return."

"Chad, we're not going to exactly rob him blind or go through with our threat or anything. I mean, it's just in fun."

"You don't think we would really show the letter

to the school board, do you?" Toad said. They were both talking at me a mile a minute. The old two-on-one tactic. We'd been using it on each other for years. "I never thought you'd be the one to back out of anything. Remember the time we scared the shit out of your sister when she and her friend were camping out in the backyard? When we made all the noises and threw all the worms in their tent? That was all your idea, if you remember, and we went along with it."

"That was different," I said. "That was my sister."

"Remember the time you made us loosen the bolts on Jim Corry's roller skates in fifth grade and he almost broke his leg."

"I didn't make you do that. You wanted to too. He wasn't supposed to get hurt."

"But we went along with you, didn't we?"

"Who's blackmailing who?" I said.

"We'll just put the screws to him for a week or so and then let the whole thing drop," B.J. said. The excitement was all over their faces.

"All for one and one for all," Toad said. "We can't do it without you, Chad. You'll spoil it for all of us if you won't go along. Besides, you were the one who found the letter in the first place. We'd never have had the evidence if you hadn't brought the letter."

"Stole it," B.J. said.

"That's a federal offense," Toad said.

"It's just for a few laughs, Chad. None of us would do anything that was really rotten or anything. You know us better than that."

"I know, but. . . ."

"Here's what we'll do. We'll try it out and if you don't think it will work or you don't like it at all, then we'll vote on it. If two of us think we shouldn't go through with it, then, fine, we won't. But let's at least plan it like we said we would. That can't hurt anybody."

They'd worn me down. As usual. "Yeah. All right," I said. "Let's plan it anyway. That'll be a kick, planning it. Then we'll vote. Okay?"

"It's going to be fantastic," Toad said. "Things couldn't have worked out any better. Mr. Patterson, for Christ's sake! And blackmail. What a perfect crime."

CHAPTER 4

After the three o'clock bell, we took the letter up to the Memorial Library in Louella and made a Xerox copy of it. That was B.J.'s idea, and it made sense.

"We'll have to show him the proof," B.J. had said. "But we don't want to let the original out of our hands."

Then we went on over to B.J.'s house. His mother was out. She worked at Altman's part time, so we settled ourselves in his rec room with the morning paper, scissors, glue, and the letter spread around us on the floor.

"We've got to make our cover letter good," B.J. said. "And we can't let him know who it's from."

"You better believe that," Toad said.

"What we'll do is this. We'll paste together a note from letters in the newspaper and tell him we want some money or we'll send the original letter to the school board. Sound all right?"

"What if he doesn't buy it?" I asked. "Suppose he just ignores it." I wasn't worried about the crime anymore, just whether it would work. I was caught up in the planning too.

"Then our illustrious career in crime comes to an abrupt end," B.J. said. "But he'll go along, all right. You don't think he'll let the school board know what we know, do you? After all, his job's at stake."

"How much do you think we should ask for in the way of money?" Toad asked. "How about a million bucks?"

B.J. didn't laugh like he usually did. "We've got to be realistic. What about a couple of hundred?"

"That's not realistic," I said. "He'd never go for that much money. No letter is worth it, not even this one."

"How much do you think?" B.J. asked.

"I don't know. Not much. It's just the principle of the thing. If we want to be sure we're successful, we can't ask for much at all."

"I'll go along with that. It makes sense."

"How about fifty bucks?" I suggested.

"Aw, fifty bucks. What kind of crime is that?" Toad said.

"I agree with Chad. But let's make it sixty. That's twenty bucks apiece, small change, but better that than nothing at all."

"You know something? We're out of our heads," I said and laughed. "I don't believe we're sitting here planning this. It'll never come off, not even for only sixty dollars."

"Sure it will. We've just got to be careful we don't leave any trails behind us. We're that smart, aren't we?"

"Besides, we've got the upper hand," Toad said. "Even if for some reason he finds out who's behind this, he can't very well turn us in. Everything would come out that way, and he sure as hell isn't going to want that to happen."

"Right. And, besides, as soon as we get the money, we'll let the whole thing drop. But, listen, you guys, if one of us does get caught, no squealing on the other two, right?"

"Right," Toad said.

"Of course," I replied.

B.J. grabbed a pencil and a piece of scrap paper. "Let's plan it out first. How should we start?"

" 'Dear Mr. Patterson,' " Toad suggested. It was just another game for him. I wasn't so sure about B.J. though.

"No way. He'd know it was a student if we said that. How about just 'Patterson.' "

"Good," I said. "We want to make sure that it could be from anyone."

"Okay, 'Patterson: You might find the enclosed letter as interesting as we did.' "

"No," I said. "We can't say 'we.' Then he'll know he's dealing with more than one person."

"Good point," B.J. said. "How about, 'Patterson: The enclosed letter is interesting. The school board would think so too, unless they already know they have hired a teacher who is mentally unstable.' "

"Mentally? How about emotionally?" I suggested.

"What do you think, Toad?"

"Emotionally is better. And how about something about not being able to handle rough situations."

"Yeah. 'And who goes to pieces under pressure.' "

"Are we going to ask for money right away?" I asked.

"Think we should?"

"We might as well. Then we can get it over with all at once."

"Don't we want him to stew for a while?" Toad asked.

"He'll sweat plenty," I said. "There's no need to be really nasty about it."

"I don't know," B.J. said. "Maybe we should just tell him that we have the letter this first time and then wait for a day or two before we ask for the money."

"We could say that instructions will follow. They always say that when they're sending ransom notes on television," Toad said.

"Jesus, Toad, this isn't exactly television," B.J. said.

"Let's make it one letter. That means less chance of having us get caught. The more letters we send, the greater the risk is going to be," I said.

"Let's vote on it," Toad said.

"No need to," B.J. said. "I agree with Chad."

"Then it's one letter."

"That's it then. What's tomorrow? Wednesday, right? Let's make sure he gets the note tomorrow and then we'll be sixty bucks richer by tomorrow night."

"We can't count on that," I said. "He may not have sixty bucks with him tomorrow. We've got to give him at least a day."

"If he doesn't have it on him, then he'll have to go to the bank on one of his free periods or over lunch or something. That's his problem. Besides, Chad, you were the one that just said you wanted to get this over with. What are you bitching about?"

"Okay, okay. It's a one-day blitz. That's just fine with me."

"What do we have so far?" Toad asked.

" 'Patterson: The enclosed letter is interesting.

The school board would think so too, unless they already know they have hired a teacher who is emotionally unstable and goes to pieces under pressure.' "

"Do we want to say something about not trying to find out who we are or the school board will get the letter immediately?" Toad asked.

"Sure."

"How about signing it?" I asked.

"Just 'x' "

"Three 'x's,' " Toad said. "He won't know what it means."

"Okay?"

"Okay," I said.

"Is that enough to start with?"

"Sounds good to me," Toad said.

"Now how about getting the money? We've got to be careful there."

"I've got an idea. I've been thinking about it since lunch," I said. "He takes the train home every day, right? Why not tell him that he should throw an envelope with money in it out of the moving train window at a certain point. Then we can make sure that no one else is checking on it."

"Like the cops?" Toad asked.

"Like the cops," I said. "You can't be sure he's not going to go to the cops."

"There's no way he would do that," B.J. said. "I can tell you, he's too uptight. You can see it all the time. If he went to the cops then the whole world would know he's a psycho. I'll make you a bet he follows through with everything we tell him to do."

"I think he will too," Toad said.

"You're probably right, but there's no sense in taking chances."

"I think the train idea is a perfect one."

"And perfection is our word," Toad said. "The train bit is fine by me."

"How will we say it?" B.J. asked.

"How about: 'The original letter will cost you sixty dollars. Place the money in a plain white envelope and throw it out the train window just as it passes over Eagle Road.' There's an empty lot there by the train bridge. We can make sure the coast is clear before we pick up the money," I said.

"Great. But we better make sure we tell him which train to be on or we could be waiting out there in the cold all afternoon."

"He took the three-forty yesterday. It goes past the empty field about three minutes later."

"Then we'll specify the three-forty train. Anything else?"

"Should we tell him where to find the letter after he's tossed the money out the window?" I asked.

"No. We can get the letter to him any time. Mail it back or something. Let's wait and see whether he's going to go through his end of the bargain first."

"Let's go to work," Toad said. He picked up the papers and the pair of scissors and we all started looking for letters to cut out to make the blackmail note. It took a hell of a long time, but it was kind of fun, looking for just the right letters. B.J. glued the letters on a piece of blank typing paper. After almost an hour we were done:

Patterson:

The enclosed letter is interesting. The School Board would think so too, unless they already know they have hired a teacher who is emotionally unstable and goes to pieces under pressure.

The original letter will cost you sixty dollars. Place the money in a plain white envelope and throw it out of the window of the Paoli local as you pass over Eagle Road.

Do not tell anyone or the letter will go to the School Board. Follow these instructions if you want your Navy record kept a secret.

xxx

I must admit we'd done a fine job. The letter looked good, the words jumping out from the page in that bold black print. It was a professional job and it showed that we meant business.

"I wish we could see his face when he opens this note," B.J. said.

"He's going to crap frogs," I said. I wished I could see it too. Any reservations I'd had about the whole prank were gone. We'd worked the whole thing out so perfectly and I didn't see how anything could go wrong.

B.J. went to his father's desk and took out a long, white envelope. He put the note and the Xerox copy of the Navy letter in and sealed it shut.

"Are we going to mail it?" Toad asked.

"No. We'll just slip it into his mailbox in the office at school. Save us a stamp that way. Besides if we're planning on getting the money tomorrow, we've got to do it that way. We can't exactly wait for the United States Postal Service to drag its feet."

"Think that's safe?" I asked.

"Sure. If we get to school real early, no one will see us."

"Who's going to put it in the mailbox?"

"Hell, I will," B.J. said. "I'm not chicken."

"And I am?" I said. B.J. smiled. "We'll go with you. We'll wait outside and make sure the coast is clear. No way are you going to do anything without us."

"Okay. Let's meet in the commons at eight tomorrow and we can take it from there." B.J. waved the envelope in the air. "Congratulations. We've done it. The perfect crime! What did I tell you guys, huh? And it wasn't hard at all."

"And we did it together. The three of us," Toad said. "Just like we said we would."

We all felt pretty good about our plans. Kind of proud, you know, and clever.

B.J. took the letter and stuck it into his notebook.

"Well, if we're all done for now, I think I'd better take off. We always have to eat early on Tuesdays. My sister's got a Girl Scout meeting," I said. I stood up and gave a short bow. "My grandfather was Al Capone, you know."

"I should have guessed. There's a family resemblance."

"Hey, Chad. How about bringing that *Playboy* with you tomorrow," Toad suggested.

"After Wednesday, you can buy your own. You'll have all that hot money to play around with," I told him.

He shot me the finger and I headed for the door.

All the way across town, I found myself grinning. I couldn't help it. Things had shaped up so well. I tried to imagine Mr. Patterson's reaction when he would read the note. I knew I'd have trouble concentrating on my homework that night. After all, it's not every day you and a couple of friends work out the perfect crime. Not a crime, really, I kept telling

myself. The perfect joke. It's not that I really dis-
liked Mr. Patterson. Not like B.J. did, anyway.
Actually, I thought he was a pretty good teacher.
We learned a lot, even if I didn't like the way he
did some things sometimes. Besides, what's sixty
dollars to a teacher? The way Mr. Patterson dressed
all the time, he had lots of money to spare.

The next few days were definitely going to be
something else. All the cloak and dagger stuff was
growing on me.

The sun was almost gone and the town was
coated in gray. All the snow had turned to slush.
I shuffled through it on the sidewalks, kicking lumps
and scattering water in front of me. Every once in
a while I stooped and made an ice ball and heaved
it at a tree. I tried pegging a squirrel that sat scold-
ing me on a branch, but I missed and it dashed
around to the other side of the trunk.

It was dark by the time I opened my front door.
My father was sitting in the living room reading the
evening paper. My sister was sitting on the floor
watching television. She had her Girl Scout uniform
on.

Dad looked up from the paper. "Hi, Chad."

"Hiya," I said. He went on back to the sports
page.

"You're almost late for dinner," Janey said.

"Tough." I put my books on the hall radiator.

Mom came out from the kitchen.

"Hi, dear," she said. "Have a good day?"

"Fine," I said. I sat down in the other easy chair
and picked up the new *Time* magazine.

"Where have you been?" Mom asked. She didn't
say it nosy or nasty like. Just asking. She always
did.

"Oh, I was over at B.J.'s. We were working on something for school." It wasn't exactly a lie. I've only really lied to my parents a couple of times and it always made me feel lousy for days.

Mom nodded. "You look concerned. Upset. Did something go wrong in school today?"

"No. Everything's fine. Just worried about a lot of homework is all."

Mom nodded again and turned back toward the kitchen. "Dinner in five minutes, everyone. Janey, come on out. It's your night to help me dish up."

"Mom, can't you wait until the show's over?"

"No, I can't. Let's go. It's your meeting we have to eat so early for."

"Just until the ad. . . ." Janey could win a nation-wide whining contest if they ever had one.

Dad dropped the paper into his lap. "Janey, you heard your mother."

Janey got to her feet and turned off the tube. She grumbled as she headed for the kitchen.

"You've got such a lovely disposition," I said as she passed.

She tried to give me a kick in the shins, but she missed. I laughed and turned to the movie reviews in *Time*. It was nice to be home.

Toad came puffing up the bus loop at a minute or two after eight. B.J. and I had been waiting for at least five minutes, pacing the commons in our wet shoes.

"Sorry, guys," he said. "My mom made me eat oatmeal. It took forever. She always has to make it from scratch. I got the leftovers for a sandwich though."

"You know something, Toad," B.J. said.

"What?"

"You're weird."

"Thanks," he said and smiled. I laughed. He always looks so dumb in his earmuffs.

"But you have a future ahead of you."

"What's that?"

"You can open a lunch counter when you grow up. Let's get moving."

We went through the corridors toward the main lobby in front of the office. The halls were empty. No one had even turned the overhead lights on, and it was dim. Only a little bit of winter sun came through the windows. Toad tried to step on every scrap of paper along the way.

"Jesus, Toad. Keep moving," B.J. said.

"You know him," I said. "Life's just one big Monopoly game."

Toad hurried up behind us, but I stayed close to B.J. so Toad couldn't step between us, forcing him to walk a pace or two behind. I got some satisfaction out of it. I didn't feel like being the odd man out again, especially since we'd decided to go through with the whole crazy plan.

Toad accidentally stepped on the back of B.J.'s heel.

"Ouch, Toad. Watch where you're walking," B.J. said.

"Sorry," Toad said and I smiled.

The glass doors of the office were still shut, but we could see Mr. Boughman behind the counter checking through a pile of cut slips from the day before. The side door to the teachers' mail room was open. Toad and I stood outside in the lobby while B.J. went to the mail-room door. He disappeared inside. Toad was shifting his weight back and forth from his right to his left leg nervously.

Just then the front door of the school opened and Mrs. Folger came in, carrying a satchel book bag, her face half hidden behind a maroon scarf. She crossed the tiled floor toward the mail room.

"Hey, Mrs. Folger."

"Morning, boys," she said and turned to face us, her back to the mail-room door.

"You know that police book I got out the other day?"

"Yes, Chad."

"Well, I'm really enjoying it. It's amazing all the stuff that cops can do to catch a criminal. Fingerprints and things." I felt really stupid standing there in the main hall, chattering away like an idiot, but I wanted her away from the door when B.J. reappeared.

"That's fine, Chad. I'm glad you're enjoying it. You could fill out a recommendation card for the file," she suggested.

"Maybe I'll do that."

"I wish you would. There are so few works of non-fiction that find their way into the box."

I glanced toward the door and saw B.J. slide out into the lobby again. He gave a short okay sign with his hand and went over to the display cases and stood there looking at the African projects the seventh graders do for humanities, a case full of papier-mâché masks and wooden and tinfoil spears.

"Well, I just wanted to tell you that I think it's a good book, Mrs. Folger. And I'll try to get it back on time for once."

Mrs. Folger smiled. "That's good. We wouldn't want to put you on our library probation list. You're too good a student for that."

"Mr. Honesty," Toad said. "That's Chad."

"I'm sure he is. Have a good day, boys," she said and crossed the lobby.

"That was quick thinking. I was paralyzed."

"So I noticed. Anyway, we're in the clear now."

"I told you we couldn't do it without you," Toad said.

B.J. came over to us. "All set. Right in the box waiting to bite him."

"Did you make sure it was the right note and not some other envelope?" Toad asked.

"Come on, Toad. What do you take me for?"

"Just checking."

"Toad doesn't have his head screwed on quite straight this morning," I said. B.J. and I started down the hall laughing over our smooth execution of the first step in our plan. Toad trailed behind.

We went back to the commons to wait for the homeroom bell, wondering the whole time whether Mr. Patterson had read the letter yet.

The first three periods dragged on forever. I couldn't keep my mind on the oil painting I was doing in art or the basketball game we had in gym. I was totally out of it during math. Mr. Proctor called on me twice and I didn't even know what the question was.

The three of us met again before fourth period, outside the English room, our trusty anthologies tucked under our arms.

"Think he's read it yet?" Toad said.

"Of course. You don't leave an envelope unopened all day."

"Think he'll take it seriously?"

"He's got to. He doesn't have any choice. You worry too much. We can just sit back and watch him sweat."

We went into the room. I don't know what I expected. I don't suppose I really thought that we would be able to read it all over his face, but I did think that something would give us a clue as to whether he had gotten the note yet or not. But there wasn't any obvious change. It seemed that maybe Mr. Patterson cut his before-class prattle with his fans a little short and called the class to order a little more quickly, but other than that I couldn't notice any difference. There were no beads of sweat standing out on his forehead or unusual shaking of his hands.

Mr. Patterson reviewed the stuff we'd read from *Paradise Lost* for homework, selections from the first and second books. And when he boomed out his melodramatic reading of Satan's suggestion to seek revenge on God by trying to undermine the Garden of Eden, not with violence, but with tricks, I almost thought he was reading it right to me:

Our better part remains
to work in close design, by fraud or guile
What force effected not: that he no less
at length from us may find, who overcomes
by force, hath overcome but half his foe,
Space may produce new worlds; whereof so rife
there went a fame in Heav'n that he ere long
Intended to create, and therein plant
A generation, whom his choice regard
Should favor equal to the Sons of Heaven. . . .
  War then, war
Open or understood, must be resolv'd.

Then Mr. Patterson read Beelzebub's speech supporting Satan's idea to destroy the Garden of Eden.

It was easy to get involved when Mr. Patterson read stuff out loud. All the poetry that seemed totally meaningless the night before when I read it for homework seemed to be real and convincing in class. That was one thing you had to say about Mr. Patterson, he had a way with words. Sometimes, just for the hell of it, he'd read a horror story to the class and he'd have you perched on the edge of your seat, shaking like a little kid having a nightmare.

Then Mr. Patterson gave us a quiz on the first two books. It was tough, but I did all right. A lot of the other kids were really squirming. I had a feeling that about half of the class hadn't even read the assignment at all. Mr. Patterson asked for a lot of names of devils and a description of hell, and we wound up writing a short essay on the quote from book one:

> The mind is its own place, and in itself
> Can make a Heav'n of Hell, a Hell of Heav'n.

I wrote almost a page on it, since it struck me as being pretty true.

The only strange thing about the quiz was, instead of playing eagle-eye and pacing the room as he usually did, just itching to catch someone cheating and hold a public spectacle, Mr. Patterson spent the whole time standing at the window, gazing out over the town, past the steeple of the Methodist Church and the bare tree branches beyond. It was lucky for B.J. too, because he copied almost every answer from me. I tried to kind of block my paper this time, not so much that B.J. couldn't see my answers, but so if Mr. Patterson did notice B.J.'s wandering eyes, he couldn't blame me this time either. Fortunately, we didn't get caught at all. Twice in a row would have finished B.J. for the year. It even occurred to me that maybe the three of us could trade the blackmail letter for A's instead of money, but I knew that would never work. But maybe it gives you an idea where my priorities lie.

On the way to lunch, B.J. was practically dancing down the stairs.

"Did you see him?" B.J. shouted. "Jesus, did you see the way he was acting? I mean, you could just tell. He was really in bad shape. He's lucky we didn't ask for a hundred bucks, then he really would be crawling. That must be the first class all year that he didn't lay into anyone, no one at all."

"He didn't look very upset to me," I said.

"Then you must be blind. Didn't you see how he wouldn't talk to anyone before class and spent most of the period staring out the window? That's not the old Mr. Patterson we know and love."

"I don't know. Maybe. I still say he didn't look all that upset to me," I said.

"Don't worry. He's as good as kissed that sixty bucks good-bye," B.J. said.

"I'm still not sure he'll have that much cash. We should have asked for even less."

"Don't worry, for Christ's sake. He'll get the money together sometime before this afternoon."

"He's bound to know that it's someone in school that's blackmailing him. You don't suppose he could suspect us, do you?"

B.J. tossed it off. "He can't even know that it's someone in our class. He can't know it's us. Besides, even if he did, it still doesn't make any difference. As long as we've got the letter, we're safe. We've got him over a barrel. There's absolutely nothing he can do about it. The power's on our side for a change. You'll see. When we get the money this afternoon, you'll both thank me."

"I'm just a little worried is all," I said.

"Don't get so upset. We're the perfect criminals, remember? What can go wrong, for God's sake? Let's get some lunch."

What can go wrong, the man says.

This time Toad walked down the steps with B.J. and it was me that trailed behind.

At three o'clock we ran through the town, up the street from school, past the shops, and under the railroad bridge on North Louella.

We crossed the fields and followed along the edge of the train embankment until we reached the overpass at Eagle Road. I don't know why we hurried so much. Excitement, I guess. By the time we got there, it was only three-fifteen and we had almost a half hour to kill before the three-forty train would carry Mr. Patterson along the tracks above us.

It was a long half hour. We sat on the damp ground surrounded by weeds and a last few patches of dirty snow. Toad, as usual, made up a game to pass the time. He plucked an old, dried milkweed stalk and we took turns seeing how long we could balance it upright on the end of our finger. There was too much wind to be very successful, so we gave it up in a hurry. Toad spent the rest of the half hour snapping the weed stalks into little pieces.

B.J. kept checking his watch. We were all kind of hyper, I guess. The anticipation was killing us. I was filled with a combination of worry and nervous happiness, like when you're a five-year-old kid at the circus watching the acrobats almost falling. The more dangerous it is, the more you love it.

"It's been fun, huh?" B.J. said. "The perfect crime bit. And we're going to pull it off just like we planned."

"I sure hope so," I said. "I just have a feeling that something is going to go wrong."

"You're out of your skull. Nothing can go wrong now." B.J. checked his watch for about the millionth time. "In five minutes when that train roars by and Patterson throws the money out the window, we're free and clear and sixty bucks richer. For the first time in my life I feel like I've accomplished something on my own. You know what I mean?"

"Yeah," Toad said, crumbling weed stalks. "I've got to admit, B.J., it's been a pretty good week. I'll almost be sorry to see it end. We've never had so much going together."

"You know it doesn't have to end," B.J. said.

"How so?" I asked. "Plan another crime?"

"Yeah, we could do that. Or we've still got the letter. We could play around with this one a little longer. I'm still not sure that Patterson's gotten everything he deserves."

Just then we heard the sound of the approaching train. We pushed ourselves against the embankment so that we couldn't be seen from the train.

"Brace yourselves, guys. Here it comes," B.J. said.

I could feel the bank vibrating against my back as the train roared by on the tracks overhead. We glanced up and about twenty yards in front of us, a white envelope fluttered out of the air. Then the train disappeared in the distance, around the bend, heading for Stratford.

B.J. jumped up, yelling at the top of his lungs,

and ran along the bottom of the embankment toward the spot where the envelope lay in the slush.

Toad and I ran after him. We stood around the envelope. It was almost anticlimactic. I mean, here was all the planning and the whole thing was over. Toad was right. It was a real downer.

B.J. reached down and picked up the envelope. "Congratulations," he said. "We did it. All of us."

"Hurry up," Toad said. "Open the damn thing."

B.J. tore the corner of the envelope and pulled out a folded piece of paper. He looked up at us. There wasn't any money. He opened up the paper. The smile dropped off his face while he read the note. His cheeks got red. Then he passed the paper over to me.

The writing on the paper said:

> To whom it may concern:
> Go screw yourself.
>   J.P.

"Some perfect crime," I said. I almost laughed.

"It's not so funny," B.J. said, and grabbed the piece of paper out of my hand. He dropped it to the ground and stomped on it, grinding it into the mud with his heel.

CHAPTER 5

As I came up the hall before fourth-period English the next day, I saw Toad leaning by the water fountain outside Mr. Patterson's room. I had stayed behind in math the period before, so most of the kids were already in the room. The halls were almost empty. Just a last few stragglers rushing toward closing doors. I didn't see B.J. around at all.

As I got closer, I could see that Toad was leaning heavily against the lockers just outside the English room. He didn't look so hot. His books were scattered on the floor. I walked over to him.

"He, Toad, what's the problem?"

He was breathing heavily. He opened his mouth, but for a second, nothing came out. Then he managed to whisper, "Listen, Chad. I feel awful."

Then he started to crumble. I don't know how to describe it. It was like all his muscles just gave way and his bones were made of rubber. He sagged down the side of the locker and ended up sprawled out on the floor. He was gasping for air.

I dropped down beside him. He was trying to say something and I couldn't hear it.

"Get somebody. I can't move."

I jumped up and rushed into Mr. Patterson's room. Mr. Patterson was up front by his desk. I ran across the room.

"Mr. Patterson! Hurry up. Toad's in the hall. Something's happened," I yelled.

Mr. Patterson turned toward me, away from the group he had been talking to. "I beg your pardon, Chad, but you're interrupting. And would you mind being a little more specific?"

"Jesus, Mr. Patterson, Toad's out in the hall. He looks like he's about to die."

That got through to him. Mr. Patterson paused for just a second more and then we hurried toward the door. Everyone started to follow. Everyone except B.J., who was standing over by the window, looking out at the gray February sky.

"Everybody sit down!" Mr. Patterson yelled and the class faltered in their rush to the door.

We ran into the hall and Toad was still on the floor, but he was sitting up, still trying to catch his breath.

Mr. Patterson knelt down beside him and placed a hand on Toad's shoulder.

"What's the matter?"

"It's okay," Toad said. "I'll be fine. I don't know what happened."

"Can you stand up?" Then Mr. Patterson turned to me. "Chad, when we get him up, start him toward the infirmary. I'll call ahead."

Mr. Patterson started to rise, but Toad reached out and stopped him.

"No, it's okay. I'll be fine. I get these every once in a while. It passes in a second."

Some color was coming back into Toad's cheeks and he did look a little better. But even so, I was worried. I mean, I'd never known anything like that to happen to him before, and, hell, we'd been friends for years, ever since I'd split his lip open by accident with a baseball bat during a baseball game.

I looked behind me and saw the rest of the class gathered in the doorway, straining to see the action.

"I thought I told you all to get into your seats," Mr. Patterson shouted. "Everything's going to be all right out here. Now get moving."

The class backed up a foot or two, but still craned their necks to find out what was going on. I couldn't see B.J. in the group. I wondered for a second why he wasn't out here helping too.

Toad started to get up. He stumbled once, but managed to grab a hold of a locker handle and get himself upright.

"Listen, it's okay. I feel fine now. Really, Mr. Patterson."

"Chad, will you get him down to the nurse. He can stretch out down there till it passes."

"No way, Mr. Patterson. I'll be all right. It's nothing, really."

I scooped Toad's books off the floor and stacked them on top of my own. Toad began to walk toward the classroom door. His steps were firmer and more sure.

"See? It always goes away quickly," he said.

"Are you sure you don't want to go down to the infirmary?" Mr. Patterson asked again. He seemed genuinely concerned, not his usual sarcastic self.

"Yeah, I'm sure. I'm fine now."

"Thanks for your help, Chad," Mr. Patterson said. We walked through the classroom door ahead of

Mr. Patterson and the group crowded there opened up to let us through.

"Okay, gang. The excitement's over. No blood, no gore. And there's no double feature today, we hope. Let's get going. We're late already and we have a lot to cover today."

I followed Toad to his seat, but he didn't seem to have any more trouble with his balance or anything. The rest of the kids spread out to their desks. B.J. was already seated in his.

"You really all right?" I asked Toad before I left for my own chair.

"Sure. It's hereditary fainting. From my maternal grandmother," he said and grinned.

He looked fine, so I went to the front of the room and slid into my desk.

"You ever see Toad have anything like that before?" I asked B.J.

"Nope. Guess he's all right now though."

"You sound concerned," I said. It was my turn to be sarcastic.

B.J. shrugged. "Like the man said, no blood, no gore. Everything's under control."

Mr. Patterson was back at his desk. He paused there and took an envelope off his blotter. He glanced up quickly at the class. Nobody else seemed to be watching him. Everybody was too busy buzzing about Toad's sudden collapse.

Mr. Patterson ripped the envelope open and took out a piece of paper. I could only see the back of it, which was blank. I kept watching while he read whatever was on it. His shoulders pulled back and the color drained from his face. I thought for a minute he was going to collapse like Toad had, but then he dropped the paper back onto the desk, opened the center drawer, and slid the paper and the envelope into it.

The class continued to chatter behind me. I heard Steve Sorrell say, "You okay, Toad?" and Toad said, "Sure, fine."

Then Mr. Patterson crossed to the little podium he had made for the front of the room.

"Enough!" he shouted. It was almost a scream. The classroom came to instant silence.

"You know what I should schedule for you?" he said. "Gladiator contests. Maybe I can arrange for a bulldozer to run over a five-year-old in the gymnasium for you. You're the kind of group that would drive a hundred miles to watch somebody jump from a fifty-story building. Well, I said the excitement's over. Do you understand? Toad's going to live, like it or not. Now I want your attention immediately."

I shifted in my seat. Something sure was wrong. I don't know whether the rest of the class sensed it or not, but then they hadn't seen him open the envelope. Even Mr. Patterson's most violent sarcasm had a glint of humor in it. This time he wasn't kidding around.

"Get your books out and open to page 47. If any of you had your ears half open, you know that yesterday we saw Satan and his little crew planning to get revenge on God by corrupting Adam and Eve in the Garden of Eden. And if any of you bothered to do your reading for homework last night, you know that he flew up out of hell to check the garden out. What we're going to look at today is God's reaction to all this. . . ."

Out of the corner of my eye, I saw B.J. raise his hand.

"Yes, B.J. Don't tell me you have a question."

"Yeah, Mr. Patterson. But not about what we read last night. Just a question in general."

"Well, what is it?" Mr. Patterson had emerged from behind the podium and was pacing in front of the first row of seats.

"Just that I don't see why we're wasting our time reading this stuff. I mean, who really cares what some guy named Milton said about Satan a couple of hundred years ago."

Mr. Patterson stopped moving. He stood still except for nodding his head.

"You know what culture is, Masterson?" Mr. Patterson said.

"Yeah. Sure."

"Well, in case you haven't noticed, we've been spending a good portion of this course trying to drum a little of it into your head. If you check the course description in your catalog, the curriculum is a survey of English literature. A little Shakespeare, a little Dickens, and right about now, a little Milton. That's what things are all about in here. It's just about the middle of February. Is it dawning on you now?"

"I know all about that, Mr. Patterson. My question isn't what we're doing in here, but why we're doing it. I mean, aren't there a lot more relevant things we could be studying than some dumb epic poem about things that have no relationship with what's going on in the world today?"

"Suppose you enlighten us all by giving us an example."

"I don't know. You're supposed to be the expert. It's just that there must be something else better than Milton."

"Is *Tubby the Tugboat* or *Tom Swift and His Electric Meatball* more your speed, B.J.?"

Steve Sorrell raised his hand.

"What, Steve? You have something to add?"

"I guess so. Isn't there some more modern stuff we could be reading? Milton's pretty old-fashioned and all, like B.J. said."

Mr. Patterson leaned back against the podium. He didn't look pleased.

"What is this, dissatisfaction in the ranks? Academic mutiny? The reason we're studying Milton and not someone else is that, believe it or not, it may just improve your power of critical thinking, heaven forbid, and increase your knowledge of your own language and maybe even teach you to read a little more effectively. Not even you, B.J., can deny the fact that if you end up a garbage collector, the skill of reading might come in handy every now and then, even if it is to read the labels on crushed soup cans."

"And another thing, Mr. Patterson," B.J. interrupted. "Milton just doesn't make any sense. I mean, in the stuff we read for today. . . ."

"Oh, you bothered to read the assignment? Is that a first for you, Masterson?"

"Check my grade average, Mr. Patterson. I do my work."

Things were getting a little rough and Mr. Patterson wasn't liking it at all. I knew now that B.J. was baiting him, but I didn't know yet whether Mr. Patterson knew it or not.

"So what didn't make sense to your tiny mind?"

"Milton has God say that whether Satan is able to corrupt Adam and Eve is up to them since they have free will, but at the same time He says that

105

he knows it's going to happen. I mean, what kind of crap is that. What sense does free will make when everything is predestined anyway?"

"The fact that God can see into the future doesn't mean that Adam and Eve's fall isn't due to their own weaknesses. Milton is saying that people lose their paradises through their own doing. Doesn't that make sense to you?"

"Suppose you've got this family, okay? And they're taking a Sunday drive to visit their poor grandmother in a nursing home. And you've got another car of, say, four teenagers driving back from the beach, and what do you know, one of the cars has a blowout and the two cars crash, and bango, everyone is dead. Is that their fault? Is that free will, huh?"

"Do you accept the consequences of your actions?" Mr. Patterson said, but before B.J. could answer, LeeAnne raised her hand.

"Yes, you too, LeeAnne?"

"Mr. Patterson. I really like what we're reading this year and all. And *Paradise Lost* is really nice and all, but there's something that bothers me about it too."

"And what's that?"

"Well, I'm not a woman's libber or anything, but I don't really like the way that Eve is described as being so inferior to Adam. I mean. . . ."

"That's what I mean, Mr. Patterson," B.J. said. "This stuff is such a load. I mean, things have changed in the last few hundred years. I don't see why. . . ."

Mr. Patterson slammed his hand down on the desk top. The shot echoed in the room and left total silence in its passing.

"You're reading it because I told you to read it. That's why. And if you don't like it, that's just too damn bad. It's the one thing you have no free will about unless, B.J., you'd like to skip *Paradise Lost* and, in that case, I would be more than happy to fail you for the term. There'll be no more discussion about it. Open your books to the selections from books five and six. Start reading. You'll have a test on the material tomorrow."

Mr. Patterson turned from his podium and went back to his desk. He sat down and glowered out across the room. It was strange; he usually liked a lively argument. He was forever playing the devil's advocate. We all buried our heads in our books in the awkward silence that followed his outburst. Beside me, I could feel B.J. gloating in his victory. I glanced up at Mr. Patterson. He had opened the desk drawer and was fingering the envelope and letter that had been on his desk at the beginning of the period.

About five minutes before the bell rang, Mr. Patterson got up from his desk and began to return the test papers from the day before. He went up and down the aisles tossing them onto the desks, but when he got to me he stopped.

"It was the best paper I've read all year," he said. He gave me the test. It was an A-plus, the only one I'd ever gotten.

"Thanks," I said.

"Don't thank me. You earned it."

He finished passing out the papers and returned to the front of the room. The twelve-ten bell rang and he said "Class dismissed" in a low, quiet voice.

We all picked up our books and started for the door. No one was saying a word.

As soon as we reached the hall and were headed toward the stairs, B.J. gave a funny little jump and clapped Toad on the back. Toad was grinning from ear to ear.

"Fantastic job," B.J. said. "You should get an Academy Award for that performance."

"Do you think they'd cast me in *The Attack of the Giant Appendix?*" Toad asked.

"What the hell's going on?" I said. "I don't understand any of this."

"My little medical emergency? Don't tell me you believed it too?"

"Me? Of course I did."

"Jesus, I'm even better than I thought. Broadway, here I come."

"I don't get it," I said. "And B.J., you really did a job on Mr. Patterson in class. What's it all about?"

"Well, while you got Patterson out in the hall, I was busy leaving another little love note on his desk. I pasted it together last night."

I pulled back from them. I was shocked, I guess. I mean, I really didn't know anything about it.

"Yeah, so I saw him open an envelope, but I thought we were going to drop the whole thing."

"You never heard me say that," B.J. said.

"He didn't come across with the sixty bucks yesterday. What makes you think it'll be any different today?"

"It'll be different. You'll see."

"You know the old saying, Chad. If at first you don't succeed," Toad said.

"Listen, I tried to call you last night, but your line was busy for hours. You've got to tell that sister of yours not to keep you out of important business. Anyway, since I couldn't get a hold of you, Toad and I just went ahead with another note, is all. Nothing's changed."

I wanted to believe that.

"We decided to double the ante, though," Toad said. "We're asking for a hundred and twenty bucks this time. It seemed sensible. We've had to go through twice the effort now. He might as well pay us twice as much. It was B.J.'s idea. Don't you think it's great?"

"What else did you put in the note?"

"It was pretty much the same kind of stuff. We told him to follow the same directions for this afternoon. We laid it on as heavy as we could about sending the letter to the school board and we said we'd release it to the local paper too. I thought that was a brilliant touch, thank you. I'll bet he's shaking in his shoes right now."

"You really think he's going to pay up, don't you?"

B.J. shrugged. "I don't care about the money anymore. Just so we make him sweat a little more. To get him back, you know. We sat out in that damn field for almost an hour yesterday."

"Is that why you were such a bastard in class today?"

"Sure. Why not? He deserves it."

"Well, I don't think I like it," I said. We were at the top of the stairs by then.

"Why not?" Toad asked. He seemed surprised I could be angry at all.

"Well, for one thing, I don't really appreciate being left out of this maneuver. I thought we were all in this together."

And that was what I was angry about, I guess. I was confused, sure, about the way things were headed, but mostly I was pissed that they could have gone off and continued without me. My anger pushed me right back into the center of it. B.J. must have known it would.

"You better believe we're still in this together," B.J. said. "Hell, don't let it bother you. We would have told you if we could have."

"Jesus, in all the years we've been friends, we've always stayed together."

B.J. put his arms around my shoulder as we went on down the stairs.

"Hey, Chad, come on now, will you. We didn't want to go ahead without you. We just had to, is all."

"I don't see why we just don't drop the whole thing. There isn't any point in it anymore."

"Sure there is. We can't just give up now when we're so close."

"And another thing," I said. "He knows for sure that whoever is sending him the notes is in our class. He's got to. It won't take him long to narrow it down to us. If I'd thought this whole thing was going to get us into trouble, I never would have gone along with it."

"There's no way he can figure out it's us. And even if he does, like we said, as long as we've got the letter, he can't do a damn thing about it. Unless he wants the whole world to know he's a psycho. Besides, there's three of us, right? And only one of him."

We reached the cafeteria. I was still mad. I don't know why. Yes, I do. The hell with Mr. Patterson; I couldn't get over the feeling of being hurt by being left out. Everything that B.J. said seemed to make some sort of warped sense, but I felt kind of betrayed or something. The least they could have done was waylay me in the halls before school to fill me in on their plans. All of a sudden I was much less concerned about what Mr. Patterson must have been feeling just then than I was about my own friendships slipping through my fingers. I wanted back in. It was the dumbest thing I could have done.

We sat down at one of the lunch tables.

"Jesus, I wish you guys had let me in on this," I said for the millionth time.

"We really did try to call you last night, Chad," Toad said. "We didn't feel right about going ahead without you. Really we didn't. Why don't you think of something now? We'll go along with you this time."

"The more he gets hassled, the more he's liable to come across with the money," B.J. said. "We've still got to keep the pressure on."

Toad unwrapped his sandwich. It was liverwurst and applesauce. I had to laugh.

B.J. and I each had a plate of school spaghetti in front of us. It made Chef Boy-ar-dee look like a gourmet cook.

"I don't know," I said. "I don't much feel like it now."

"Hey, come on, will you? It would make us feel better, Chad. Then we won't feel bad about not getting you in on the stuff this morning."

"We'll help if you want," Toad said.

"Why don't we just see if he comes across with the money this afternoon. If he doesn't, I say we drop it. There's no point in carrying this too far."

"Maybe. But I hate to see us ease up before this afternoon. Listen, he's over there on lunchroom duty right now. It's our last chance for a final push."

"Why don't you think of something, Chad? Just one more thing. Then we'll all be evened up again."

"Gotta earn your share of the pot," B.J. said.

"I don't feel like it."

"He doesn't feel like it. Aw, too bad," B.J. said. "We go to all the extra trouble last night and this morning, and you get your chance to prove yourself, and you don't feel like it."

"Why don't you feel like it?" Toad asked.

"I just don't."

"If you are so damned concerned with not being left out of this deal, then you had just better join in again. I thought you had more loyalty than to just give up."

"Why don't you go up to him and tell him you know a good psychiatrist if he ever needs one," Toad said.

"Funny man."

"You could tell him that you just saw a huge Saint Bernard running across the school field with a letter in its mouth."

"You know what I like about you two?" I said. "Your subtlety."

"We got the light touch all right," B.J. said. "Come on, Chad. I mean, we've been through too much together for you to pull away now. It's just not like you. You've never been like this before. You've always been a good sport. We need you in on this. Don't we, Toad?"

"Jesus, yes. You weren't really mad at us, were you?"

"One last push. Then the money this afternoon. And then it's over and done with."

"We could stage an accident or something," I said, against my better judgment.

112

"Another medical emergency? He'd never buy it," B.J. said.

"No, I was thinking of some other kind of accident."

"Keep thinking," B.J. said. "You're getting somewhere."

"Oh, I don't know. Forget it. We shouldn't do anything else. Enough's enough."

"You know how much he loves his clothes?" B.J. said.

"Good Lord, he probably spends five dollars for each pair of jockey shorts," Toad said.

"Well," B.J. suggested. "Maybe we could pull off your usual everyday lunchroom spill. Only it's Patterson that happens to be in the way."

"Now that's the kind of accident we like to hear about," Toad said. "He'll go berserk."

"No doubt," B.J. said.

"Oh, come on, you guys," I said. They weren't listening.

"Okay, here's how we can make it work. It's got to look completely like an accident. Toad, you walk alongside of Chad. He can carry his tray. When you get next to Patterson, I'll shout your name, Chad, like I want you for something. You spin around, drop your tray, and that's that."

"God, is he going to be mad," Toad said.

"Count me out," I said.

B.J. turned to me. "I really don't believe you, Chad. I never thought I'd see the day when you'd chicken out. If I remember correctly, it was only a few days ago when we agreed that we were all in this together."

"I'll watch, okay? I'll be the one to shout your name, B.J. You can drop the tray. It was your idea."

113

"You don't seem to recall that it was you who suggested some sort of accident."

I felt pinned to the wall. You can't back out on your best friends. It just isn't easy to do.

"I tell you what we'll do. We've been in this together. We'll make this fair. We'll draw straws. Okay?"

"I don't know," I hesitated.

"Good. Be right back."

B.J. jumped up from the table and ran up to the lunch counter. I watched him as he grabbed three straws from the carton by the cashier and hurried back toward us.

When he got back to the table, he scattered the three paper straws in front of him. He picked one up and tore it in half, then he whisked up the other two and held all three in his fist with just the tops of the straws sticking up.

"Short one carries the tray. You can't get much fairer than that."

Toad drew first. It was a long straw. I picked second. Of course it was the short one. Talk about poetic justice again. I still wanted to back out, but I knew I couldn't.

"You'll carry the tray?" B.J. asked.

"I guess. I guess I have to."

B.J. looked at me. He raised one eyebrow. "Thanks, Chad. I was afraid there that you were going to pull out on us. You're too good a friend. I'm glad you're still with us."

"I wouldn't pull out," I said.

"I should hope not. Jeez, I told B.J. you wouldn't."

"Besides," B.J. smiled. "You're in as far as we are now."

I picked my tray off the table, the plate still full of spaghetti. I'd taken a bite or two, but it tasted like it always did, like someone had cooked shoe laces in a vat of rotten tomatoes. Toad came with me and we crossed the cafeteria toward the counter where the trays were supposed to be dumped. Mr. Patterson was standing near the lunch line, trying to keep kids from butting in. The noise was roaring around me and sweat was dripping down the back of my neck. Heat and noise, that's what the cafeteria was made of.

"Listen, Chad. Did you see the movie on Six last night?"

"No, I missed it."

"Well, it was really something. This guy knows that the Mafia is after him, see, because he. . . ."

We were close to Mr. Patterson by then, almost in front of him. Toad was on my left and Mr. Patterson would be on my right. I was looking at Toad, nodding idiotically at his prattle, just as we walked by Mr. Patterson.

"Hey, Chad," B.J. shouted.

I turned and bumped into Mr. Patterson.

"Get me an ice cream sandwich, will you?" I heard B.J. say in the distance, but it was drowned out by the sound of crashing dishes. The collision was perfect; the tray dipped and the dishes slipped forward and dumped themselves down the front of Mr. Patterson's pants. At the sound of the breaking dishes, a cheer rose up in the cafeteria. It always did when someone dropped a tray.

I glanced up at Mr. Patterson and then down at his pants, dripping wormy spaghetti and rancid tomato sauce. The heat and the roar of noise were overpowering.

"Gee, I'm sorry, Mr. . . ." I started to say.

I didn't have a chance to finish. Mr. Patterson grabbed me by the front of my shirt.

"You bastard," he hissed. His eyes were wide open and his mouth was tight closed, his lips almost white. He looked angry. And hurt.

"Listen, I didn't. . . ."

He grabbed my shoulder and shoved me, turning, and I spun backwards into a pillar. Just before the back of my head smashed against the column, I could see everyone in the cafeteria looking in our direction. Toad just stood there, his face amazed, shuffling a little from side to side. I heard a few kids shouting "Fight! Fight!" People in the back were standing up to see better.

A white flash buzzed in front of my eyes when my head hit the tile. Then he was at me again, grabbing my arm this time. I saw his other hand rise and then, I tried to duck when I saw the punch coming. He smashed me openhanded across the face. I thought for a second that I heard my teeth clicking together. Then he hit me again from the other direction. I could feel the blood rush to my cheeks and the heat where the hand had left its marks.

I threw my arm across my face trying to block another slap, but there wasn't one.

I opened my eyes and shook my head. Mr. Patterson was still standing in front of me, but so was B.J. B.J. had Mr. Patterson's arm held in his two hands, pulling against the force of the slap.

"Jesus, stop it, Mr. Patterson," B.J. said.

Mr. Patterson's arm relaxed in B.J.'s grasp and he stepped a foot or two back and looked at me. There was a funny blankness in his eyes. I looked down.

Mr. Patterson shook his arm free from B.J.'s hold.

"Jesus, why'd you hit him?" B.J. was saying. "It was just an accident. For God's sake. You're not allowed to hit kids in this school. Didn't anyone ever tell you that?"

Mr. Patterson's eyes shifted from my face to B.J.'s.

"There was no reason to hit Chad. He didn't do it on purpose."

Mr. Patterson looked down at the mess dripping from his pants and the broken plates on the floor. His eyes reflected the overhead light.

"Don't you know you can't hit students? Jesus, Mr. Patterson, you must be crazy."

Mr. Patterson looked at B.J. again. B.J. smiled. It sent a chill down my back. My head ached like fury.

Patterson nodded once, and then turned away from us. He walked quickly to the cafeteria door, went into the hall, and disappeared from view. A few catcalls and whistles followed him out the door.

B.J. turned to me. "Beautiful. That was beautiful."

"My head hurts," I said.

"Who said crime wasn't dangerous," he said and laughed.

Toad slapped my back and the three of us went back to our table for the rest of the lunch hour. B.J. and Toad talked like crazy about what they were going to do with the money. I didn't say a word.

CHAPTER 6

We were behind Mr. Patterson as he walked up North Louella Avenue toward the train station after school that day. We stayed pretty far back. You better believe we didn't want to take any chances being seen.

He stopped in at the liquor store again. The last time I had seen him go in seemed like a million years ago instead of just a few days.

"He must be planning to drown himself in drink," Toad said.

"I think we're beginning to get to him," B.J. said. "He'll drop the money off today. In this morning's note I told him the procedure was the same."

"You mean we're going to have to spend another freezing half hour in the cold?" I said. I wasn't looking forward to it.

"Yeah. But you figure at forty bucks an hour, it's pretty good money. Unless you want to go on over to him and ask him outright for the cash. Be my guest."

I laughed.

"Yeah, laugh it up. But if you freeze your ass off,

blame it on yourself. The train idea was yours, remember?"

"Okay, okay. I'm sorry I mentioned it," I said.

Mr. Patterson came out of the state store with a brown bag under his arm. He continued on up the street to the train station.

We dashed under the overpass and out onto the North Louella field, followed the line of the tracks the way we had done the day before. We got to the same spot and settled down to wait. I could see the muddy footprints we had already made.

I checked my watch. We didn't have as long to wait. Just a few more minutes would bring the train roaring along above us and the white envelope with the money would come flying out of the window and the whole deal would be over for once and for all. Why didn't Mr. Patterson just give in and get it over with? He must know that we meant business. I couldn't understand him being so goddamn stubborn.

Toad squatted on his haunches to keep the bottom of his pants from getting wet. He tied knots in the weed stalks instead of picking them to bits.

"Just want to see how many knots I can tie in one weed," he explained. The most he got was five before the brittle stalks broke and he had to start all over again.

B.J. paced. He kept licking his lips and you could see that he was getting more and more worked up.

I checked the sky. It looked like another storm was coming. The temperature was dropping fast and the wind was picking up. The weatherman that morning had predicted snow before dark. If we were lucky, maybe we'd get a snow day yet.

I was shaking. And not completely from the cold.

I found myself chanting silently to myself: please, let him throw the money. Please, let's get it over with. All I wanted was the nightmare to end so the three of us could go back to our normal, humdrum lives. I didn't like B.J. as much as I had the week before, and I was beginning to dislike myself more and more too. It didn't seem like too much to ask, just to have everything back the way it had been before.

Then I heard the sound of the train accelerating from the Louella Station and we pushed ourselves into the embankment again. The train rumbled by overhead and we looked up, waiting for the white envelope to come tumbling out of the sky.

But there was no envelope. There was nothing but the gray clouds above us and the sound of the engine disappearing in the distance.

"Shit," B.J. said. "I don't believe it. We can't do a simple thing like this right."

"Maybe he wasn't on the train. Think we should wait for the next one?" Toad suggested.

"Of course he was on the train. We saw him go up to the station, didn't we?"

"Yes."

"I can't believe he's that dumb. I was sure we had it made. Jesus Christ," B.J. shouted as loud as he could and kicked the embankment. "He just isn't going to play along with us. He's still not ready yet."

"The guy's a real masochist," Toad said. "He's a little slow to get the point."

"He'll get it. Don't worry."

"We're dropping it," I said. "We agreed on that."

"Not now. It's too late for that," B.J. said. "Jesus, I'm tired of your backing down all the time. Come off it, will you? Just for once, let's finish something all the way."

"What are we going to do?" Toad asked. He was ready for anything.

"Show us where he lives, Chad."

"What?"

"You heard me. Show us where he lives. You followed him home, didn't you? That's what started this thing."

"Yeah. I followed him."

"So show us."

"What for?"

"Are you going to demand the money?" Toad said.

"You'll see."

"Listen, B.J. It's over. We agreed."

"You agreed."

"I won't take you then."

"You're going to pull one of those, huh? Fine. I'll find it myself. Stratford Station Apartments you said. It should be easy. Are you coming, Toad?"

Toad glanced at me briefly, then turned away. "Sure. I wouldn't miss it."

They climbed up and away from me toward the top of the embankment. The quickest way to Stratford was along the railroad tracks. The apartments were only a mile or so away.

When they got to the top of the bank they stopped and looked back. Then they began to move down the tracks. I could see Toad jumping from tie to tie. Always a game.

I started up the embankment after them in the fading light. I couldn't let them go without me.

I followed along about twenty yards behind, listening to them joking and laughing as they headed west. Once we had to jump off the tracks into the bushes on the side. A freight rushed by for almost five minutes and almost swept me along in its rush of air. The sound pounded my ears and left my head numb when it had passed. I don't ever want to be that close to a train again.

We reached Stratford Station in about fifteen minutes. Toad and B.J. ran down the rickety station steps. I paused for a second and then descended after them. They ran past the green Victorian station building and across Old Eagle School Road. They passed the blue sign that said STRATFORD STATION APARTMENTS and I stayed about twenty yards back.

Finally, they paused at the edge of the sidewalk and waited for me.

"I knew you'd come," B.J. said. "Which way?"

I glanced across the lawn that led behind the first row of buildings.

B.J. turned and started across the open space in the direction that my eyes had glanced. Toad hurried to keep up with him. I followed.

B.J. paused behind the buildings.

"Which one is his?"

I didn't say anything.

"Goddamn it, Chad, which one is Patterson's?"

"I think it's that one," I said, pointing to the window of the basement apartment just ahead.

It was getting dark. The wind was rising and a few flurries snapped at us out of the sky. The window was lit and the orange light spilled out onto the brown lawn.

"Good," B.J. said. "He's there. And he can't see us out here if we stay out of the light."

"What's the idea?" I asked.

"This," B.J. said and pulled a can of black spray paint out of his parka pocket.

"Where'd that come from?" Toad said.

"I used a magic word and turned my glove into it," B.J. said. "I just had the feeling that he wouldn't come through with the money today. I picked this up in the janitor's closet just in case."

"You had this planned all along?" I said.

"Well, not the whole thing maybe. But I had my suspicions."

"I'll tell you, B.J.," Toad said. "I've got to hand it to you. You don't mess around. What are you going to do with it?"

"Watch," he said and crept up toward the window. Toad followed and I stepped a pace or two behind.

B.J. uncapped the spray can and shook it until the little ball inside began to rattle. He gave it a little trial *whist*. The black paint spurted out and disappeared in the growing darkness.

We were almost at the window, just beyond the overhang from the terrace of the apartment above. There was a patch of gravel in front of the window. B.J. stepped on it, ducking low to get underneath the terrace above. The gravel made a crunching sound and I jumped.

We could see in the window. There was a living room light on, but no one in sight. On the other side of the living room was a dining area with a table and some chairs. Around the other side of a wall came the bright fluorescent light of a kitchen. Shadows passed back and forth on the wooden floor. Mr. Patterson had to be in there making dinner or something.

B.J. started to spray. He started at the right side

and made a big half circle, then closed it with a vertical line. Next he made a swirling snake shape, moving toward the left from the first shape. I couldn't tell what it was supposed to be.

I wanted B.J. to hurry so he could get finished and move ass back to Lancaster Pike and we could hitch on home. I didn't much like this hanging around in the dark. If someone came along and spotted him vandalizing the place, we'd be in real trouble. I expected a voice to yell out, "Hey, kids, what are you up to?" but there was nothing but the wind and the soft sound of snow flakes against the nylon of my jacket.

B.J. drew a huge forked shape to the left of the snake. Then another half circle, a goal-post shape and then he was just filling in a giant circle when the light in the kitchen snapped out.

"Jesus," I said, "let's go." B.J. stood there finishing his circle until the completed shapes stood out boldly in their blackness:

OHƆYƧ9

"Hurry up," I shouted, but B.J. started on an exclamation point.

"He can't see us out here," he said. "And even if he sees that someone's here, he'll never be able to tell who it is."

Then Mr. Patterson came around the corner from the kitchen. He stepped into the dining area and stood there looking up at the window. He had jeans on and a sweater and had a drink in his hand.

He froze there while B.J. put the final dot on the exclamation point, pulling his face back out of the light while he did it. All Mr. Patterson would be able to see would be a pair of legs. And the huge black letters.

Mr. Patterson rushed toward the window. His mouth was open as if he were yelling, but I couldn't hear whether he was saying anything or not. B.J. jumped back from the window, bumping his head on the terrace above. He stumbled, fell down, and Toad grabbed for him, half pulling, half stumbling with him further into the darkness.

I kept watching the window. I couldn't move. Mr. Patterson still seemed to be yelling as he rushed toward me, grabbing a wooden chair as he ran.

Behind me, B.J. got to his feet. He was swearing a blue streak, rubbing his head. Toad kept saying, "You all right? You all right?"

I glanced back into the window just as the chair came flying at me. Then there was glass everywhere. The window exploded into a thousand pieces and bits of it flew by my head and clattered on the gravel. The chair was half wedged in the window frame.

I felt a stinging along the side of my cheek and the warmth of blood dripping on my neck.

Still the glass seemed to be soaring around me. It sparkled in the reflected light and seemed to coast in slow motion. The glass and the snow flakes was a strange and beautiful combination.

"Jesus Christ, Chad, come on!" Toad yelled and then we were off. We ran down the line of the apartment houses. There was a kind of roaring as we fled, the sound of the wind in our ears.

We ran onto Lancaster Pike into the street light and car light. We ran up the rise toward Louella. We kept running until we reached the Stratford Shopping Center and then we stopped to get our breath. I looked behind us. Mr. Patterson hadn't tried to follow. We just stood there, panting.

"I think we'll get our money tomorrow," B.J. said. "I don't think we'll have to do anything else. Like I promised, Chad. He's on the edge of giving in."

"Yeah," Toad said, puffing. "How about that. I'd just about given up hope."

I reached my hand up and brushed my cheek. The blood had stopped, but when my hand passed across the spot, a sharp pain flashed up the side of my face.

"Hey, Chad," Toad said. "You're bleeding."

"Smart man," I said. It was about time they noticed.

"Come on over here in the light," B.J. said. Toad and I crossed until we were standing directly beneath a street lamp.

"It's not so bad," B.J. said. "Just a scratch. I bet my head hurts more than that does."

"Then I feel sorry for you," I said sarcastically. "Is there something in it?" I brushed my cheek again and the sharp pain was still there.

Toad leaned forward. "It's hard to see with all the blood." He squinted up his little piggy eyes and leaned closer. "Yeah, just a second." He reached up and plucked a small piece of glass from my cheek. He showed it to me. I could feel the blood starting again.

"You better go home and get that cleaned up," Toad said. "It's just a little cut though."

126

"Hey, maybe you'll get a scar. Won't that be something. Old Scarface himself," B.J. said.

"Very funny," I said. "What the hell am I going to tell my parents? What the hell are we doing any of this for? Jesus, I don't believe you guys. I really don't."

"Tell your parents you cut yourself shaving," B.J. suggested.

"Go screw yourself," I said. "You're both out of your minds. I don't want anything more to do with it."

"Touchy, touchy. Well, let's get moving. It's been some kind of afternoon. Tomorrow we celebrate."

We walked the rest of the way back to town. My cheek stopped bleeding again and the pain went away. The cold, wet flakes felt good. I was so tired, all I wanted to do was curl up in the snow and go to sleep.

When we got back to the center of Louella, we split up, B.J. and Toad saying good-bye under the light of the street lamp on the main corner.

"Tomorrow we score," B.J. yelled. "I can guarantee it."

He sounded so sure. I ran the rest of the way to my house, feeling the snow hit my face and gather on my eyelids, hoping it would wash away some of the blood and the image I had of Mr. Patterson's face as he threw the chair at the window.

The snow did a better job on the blood.

I stepped through my front door and took off my coat in the hallway. I could see my parents sitting in the living room having their nightly cocktail.

"That you, Chad?" Dad asked.

"Yeah," I replied.

"Come here a second. Your mother and I want to talk with you."

"Just a minute," I said. "I have to run upstairs. I'll be right down."

I dashed for the stairs, keeping my torn cheek turned away from the light.

"Whatever it is, it can wait," my father was saying as I ran up the steps. "Come in here."

"I'll be right down," I shouted back. I reached the top of the stairs and went into the bathroom. As I flicked on the light and shut the door, I could hear my sister crying behind the door to her bedroom.

I looked in the mirror. My face was a mess. The snow-diluted blood crusted my cheek and neck. I took my shirt off and threw it in the hamper. I wet a washrag with hot water and scrubbed at the blood. When it was all washed away, the cut didn't look so bad. I had been afraid I'd need a few stitches, but now, in the harsh light of the bathroom, I could see that it was a small gash, only a half-inch long. A small corner of skin hung down like a flap. I took some alcohol out of the cupboard and poured it into the hole. The cold liquid ran down my face and it hurt like hell. I appreciated the pain. I stood there, waiting for it to pass. I pulled a large Band-Aid out of the medicine box and stuck it over the wound. The first one didn't stick. My face was still too wet, but the second one held.

I left the bathroom and crossed the hall to my room. My sister was still crying. She had her record player on, trying to drown out her sobs, but it wasn't working. I pulled a clean shirt out of a drawer, kicked off my wet shoes, and went back downstairs.

My father was standing at the bar, pouring another round of drinks for Mom and him. It's always been their time, cocktail hour. Even when Janey and I were little, we knew it was their time. We could be with them, listening in or playing quietly on the floor, but we knew from the start that if we complained, or fought, or bitched, that we'd be banished until dinner. There were plenty of times which were our times: all day Saturday and most of Sunday too when we'd all lie on the floor around the comic pages or pack a picnic lunch, but cocktail time was adult time and children were just not allowed to intrude. So I wondered what the emergency was. Something that couldn't wait until dinner was something pretty important.

"Sorry," I said, as I came into the living room. "I had to go up to the bathroom and patch up my face."

"What happened?" Mom asked.

"Oh, nothing. I slipped on some ice coming home and took a hunk out of my cheek. It's not bad." A lie again. I didn't like it. I was getting pretty sick of dishonesty.

"Let me see," my mother said, sitting forward in her chair.

"Don't worry. I'm not permanently disfigured," I said and grinned, trying to look like nothing was bothering me. The smile stretched my cheek and it hurt.

"Think Dr. McLloyd should take a look at it?" Mom asked.

"No. It's just a small crater."

Dad brought the drinks over to the coffee table and sat down in his chair, his favorite. No one else dared to sit in it. I always enjoyed watching Dad squirm when an unknowing guest sat there. I don't think Dad was really comfortable in any other chair in the house. I sat down in the love seat opposite him.

"What's to talk?" I asked.

"Have you ever cheated?" my father asked. "In school?"

God, a million thoughts raced through my brain. Why would he ask me that at that very moment? Had Mr. Patterson known it was us all along? Had he reported us? What kind of cheating was my father talking about?

"Yes," I said. And then to cover myself, I said, "Every once in a while, I guess. On a little quiz or something. A lot of people do at one time or another."

"You see," Mom said. "I told you."

My father nodded. He didn't look especially pleased with my answer. He didn't look surprised either.

"Have you ever been caught?" he asked.

"Yes. A couple of times." I had to tell him. I was too tired of deceit. "Last week I got an F on an English test for cheating. Only it wasn't me. Somebody was looking off my paper and Mr. Patterson caught him. He flunked us both."

"That doesn't seem entirely fair," Mom said. "B.J., no doubt."

I nodded.

"I can understand the teacher failing you both," Dad said. "Why didn't you tell us?"

I shrugged. "I thought I'd just try to make it up on my own." I was still worried. I couldn't understand why we were having this conversation out of the blue. It wasn't something we usually talked about. I think my parents pretty much assumed that my sister and I were trustworthy and knew what was the best thing to do.

"What's this all about?" I asked.

"Janey brought a note home with her that we have to sign and send back with her tomorrow. It's from her math teacher. Janey was caught cheating on a test today. The note explains the circumstances and says that it means an F on the test."

"Yeah?"

"Well, your father and I have been discussing what we should do about it. Dad thinks we should take away her television for a week, but I feel that the failure is punishment enough. She was very upset. Now that we know that you've cheated occasionally too. . . ."

My father interrupted her. "Because Chad has cheated doesn't make it any more acceptable that Janey has too."

"And a lot of other people too," I said. I don't know why I felt I had to justify myself.

"That doesn't make it right. I think Janey's getting off easy if we keep her away from the television for a week," Dad said. "I don't want this to be easy on her. And I don't want it to happen again. That goes for both of you."

"Of course, we don't want to make it easy on her," Mom said. "But considering this is the first time it's happened, and she is so upset. Is she still upstairs crying, Chad?"

"Yes."

"You see, dear. I'm sure she's learned her lesson."

My father turned to me. "What do you think, Chad?"

I knew what I wanted to say. It wasn't what I thought my father expected to hear, but, after the last week, it was exactly the way I had come to feel.

"I think you ought to take away the television. If someone had done that to me the first time I cheated, even if it was just on a little quiz or something, then maybe I wouldn't have gotten the F last week." Or gotten involved in some goddamn blackmail plot and been crueler to Mr. Patterson than any human has a right to be to any other human being, I wanted to say; but I didn't. "I think you ought to punish her."

"I'm glad you said that, Chad. It makes me feel a little better about you as well. I'd like to think we've raised children who are basically honest," Dad said. "And don't worry, dear," he said to Mom. "I'll play the ogre and break the news to her. I think she'd be disappointed in us if we just let it slide."

Dad crossed to the bottom of the stairs and yelled, "Janey, come down here for a moment, please."

In a minute, Janey arrived at the top of the steps wiping her eyes. They were all red and ugly. She'd had some afternoon too.

She came down the stairs and stood at the bottom, facing us in the living room.

"What?" she asked.

"Your mother and I will sign the note, but because we want you to understand the consequences of your action, you're not to watch television for a week. Maybe next time you're tempted to cheat, you'll consider what the outcome might be."

Janey just turned and ran back upstairs, crying again in great whooping sobs.

"Okay?" Dad said.

"I think we made the right decision," Mom said.

"And we can't give in and let her have the TV back after a day or two."

"Granted."

"Thanks, Chad," Dad said. "I appreciate your help."

"That's okay."

My mother turned to me. "Now tell us why you're upset."

"What?" I said.

"Something's bothering you. It has for a few days. Do you feel like sharing it with your father and me?"

"It really shows, huh?"

"Yes. Can we help?" my father said.

"I don't think so," I said. "I wish I could tell you, but I can't. You'll have to trust me."

"We always have."

"It's something at school. Something that didn't work out the way it started. It'll be all over tomorrow."

"Good."

"I've decided to return something that doesn't really belong to me."

I hadn't realized that that was what I had decided until I said it out loud. In fact I think I'd made the decision the moment the window had shattered, but I hadn't realized it then. I felt a little relieved already.

"I've got some homework to do," I said. "Call me when dinner is ready."

"I hope it all works out," Dad said.

"It will. I hope."

I went back upstairs and sat at my desk and opened my English book to the homework assignment in *Paradise Lost*. But I couldn't read it. I just sat there, looking out the window, thinking about what I had to do.

CHAPTER 7

When my alarm went off, I jumped out of bed and ran to the window. The sky was clear and only a thin powder of white graced the grass and street.

I got dressed slowly.

I had had a dream which I remembered when I was in the bathroom. Satan was in it and Toad and B.J. and me and Mr. Patterson and it all took place in the Garden of Eden, but when the wind blew, the leaves made the sound of breaking glass.

When third period was over, I hurried to English. I dashed up the stairs from the math center and pushed my way through the crowds in the halls. I didn't want to meet Toad or B.J. I wanted to get into the room and take my seat so I wouldn't have to face them. I was afraid I would change my mind.

I almost did a couple of times during class.

I was in the room before almost everyone else. Only LeeAnne had beaten me. She was up front at Mr. Patterson's desk as usual, shaking her head and talking a mile a minute. Probably about what her grade would be. I don't know what he could say to her, but she always asked.

I looked up at Mr. Patterson and he glanced my way. I quickly lowered my head and slunk into my seat. The events of the night before didn't show on his face. Other than the cut, I was hoping they didn't show on mine either.

Mr. Patterson seemed as cool and collected as usual as he heard LeeAnne dribble out her spiel. As I sat there, watching him, I wondered again whether my decision was the right one. Maybe B.J. had had Mr. Patterson pegged all along and he did deserve everything we had handed out to him. But I couldn't really believe that.

The rest of the class filed in by ones and twos. B.J. sat down in the seat beside me.

"Hiya," he said. "All recovered?"

I nodded. I didn't trust myself to speak. I kept wondering whether Mr. Patterson sensed the significance of the Band-Aid still on my cheek. It was foolish thinking, of course; he could have no way of knowing that his flying glass had cut me.

"We'll get the money today," B.J. said. "No way he can hold out any longer."

"You don't give up, do you?" I said.

"No way. I made up one last note, telling him to throw the money today or else. Why don't we sneak it into his mailbox after lunch?"

"Sure, why not?"

"He won't be expecting it there. I think trying to get it up to his desk like yesterday would be too risky."

I nodded again. I felt like an idiot and hoped the class would start soon.

"You seem a little strung out, Chad. Listen, don't worry. He couldn't have seen us last night. And after today, it'll all be over. Then we can move on to bigger and better things." B.J. laughed. "How about the First National Bank?"

LeeAnne returned to her seat behind me and Mr. Patterson walked to the front of the room.

"If you did your reading last night, then you know Milton's version of that ancient tale of the snake in the grass. Too bad about the Garden of Eden. It must have been a nice place. Too bad all good things seem to pass. What I want to talk about today is what made Eve and then Adam succumb to Satan's pressures. The question is: When you've got the whole thing made for you, why would you be tempted by anything else?"

Steve Sorrell raised his hand. "Maybe they didn't know they had everything they could have ever wanted."

"But they knew that. God told them."

"Oh, sure they had been told, but is that good enough? I mean, unless they had had any hardship, they wouldn't have anything to compare their happiness to. They couldn't have known that there was nothing better."

"Interesting point, Steve," Mr. Patterson said. The discussion was on.

"Yeah," LeeAnne said, "but they did know there had to be something more. I mean, why would God have warned them away from the tree. They must have known that too. It was the Tree of Knowledge, after all. That must have made them curious."

"Both of them? Did both Adam and Eve break God's wishes for the same reason?" Patterson asked.

"Of course not. Eve sinned because the devil tempted her. And Adam ate the fruit of the tree because Eve had and he loved her. He couldn't leave her alone in her punishment."

B.J. raised his hand.

"Yes, B.J.?" Mr. Patterson said.

"It's very simple. Eve ate the apple because she wanted power. That's the key, after all. Satan said it would make her like a goddess. Who can resist that? If you've got the choice between remaining dumb and ignorant all your life, and gaining knowledge and power, of course someone, anyone, would bite the apple."

"Do you think that's true, B.J.?"

"Yes. I don't care how content you are with the way things are, you have to take the risks to go further."

"No matter what might happen?"

"No matter what might happen. Absolutely. You have to be a fool to be happy with what you have forever."

"Do you agree, Chad?"

"I don't know, Mr. Patterson. Maybe B.J.'s right. But sometimes I think I'd rather be dumb and ignorant and happy than smart and insecure and sad. Besides, what Eve did, didn't hurt only herself. That might have been different. It hurt Adam. He had to go along with her. And if you believe what Milton said, it passed on original sin for all of us."

"I'll tell you who was the dumb one," B.J. said. "It was Adam. So Eve broke the rules. That's no reason for him to go along with her. After all, he's got a lot more ribs tucked away inside. He should have told her to stuff it and asked God for a new broad."

Everyone laughed out but Mr. Patterson and me. I could hear Toad yucking it up behind me.

"Seriously, B.J., you don't think Adam's love for

Eve was enough to justify his following in her foot-steps?"

"Of course not. Just because someone you like does something doesn't mean you have to go along with it. Unless you want the power too."

B.J. looked my way and gave me a quick smile. I couldn't tell if he was being sarcastic or not.

"I don't know," I said. "I think a lot of people would go along with someone they liked even if it meant they'd be hurt in the long run."

"Then some people are dumber than I am," B.J. said.

"Do you think Milton was right about passing all this on down the ages?" Mr. Patterson said.

"Yeah, I think he was," I said. "It always seems like the good times never last."

"I know what you mean, Chad," Mr. Patterson said. "Steve, what do you think?"

Steve said, "Well, in a sense, they didn't really lose paradise. Milton says, and the Bible too, that Christ was planning to sacrifice himself for man-kind and paradise would be regained. I mean, I guess you don't completely lose if someone is will-ing to sacrifice themselves for you."

Then Steve started back on the original sin idea and my mind began to wander. I really didn't listen much after that. All the talk about *Paradise Lost* was making me sad. I mean, all that perfection down the drain. I kept going over in my mind what I was going to do after class, and what I was going to say. But although I didn't hear much of what was being said, I did watch Mr. Patterson perform.

He wasn't quite the same person that he was a week ago. As I sat there and really studied him, I could tell that things had changed. Sure, he looked pretty much the same on the outside and he still paced the room, slinging out names and tough questions and always fielding someone's answer with the opposite view, no matter what the opinion was.

His hair was all neat and trimmed as usual, and his knit pants had just the right belt and matching tie. His jacket was slung over the back of his chair just as it always was.

But there was a difference. The eyes, for instance. Mr. Patterson was the kind of teacher who could stop a kid from talking just by looking at him. You'd be leaning over to crack a joke with your neighbor or something and you'd glance up and Mr. Patterson would be staring right at you, his eyes not flickering a bit. Your tongue just curled up in your mouth and played dead. But as I looked at him, his eyes weren't like that anymore. They darted around, like birds. Even when he was listening to what someone was saying, his eyes wouldn't stay in one place.

His hands were different too. First they were on the podium, then brushing back his hair, then stuck in his pockets. Like his eyes, his hands didn't stop once during the rest of the period.

I don't care what B.J. had said, Mr. Patterson had changed. If you looked real close, you could see exactly how much we had gotten to him and just how unfair it was.

B.J. had changed too. I glanced over at him and he was slouched back in his chair, kind of half smiling, looking pleased with himself. I think the whole week had gone to his head. He loved being in the driver's seat for a change and it didn't do him any good.

And Toad had changed. And I guess I had too.

The class wound down to a close and I hadn't gotten a thing out of the last half of it. I could only remember bits and pieces of the rest of the discussion.

"Dismissed," Mr. Patterson said, and we all got our books together and headed for the door.

Out in the hall I turned to Toad and B.J.

"You guys, go on down to lunch. I'll be down in a few minutes. I've got a math book I left in the math center. I have to pick it up. Save me a seat, will you?"

"We'll go with you," Toad said.

"Nah, don't worry about it. Better get a table for us. It'll only take a sec."

B.J. just looked at me. He didn't say anything. Then he nodded once and he and Toad went on down the hall toward the stairs. When they turned the corner and disappeared, I hurried down the corridor to where our lockers were.

I stopped in front of B.J.'s and spun the dial on the combination lock. We all knew each other's combinations. It didn't make any difference that the homeroom teacher advised us against giving our combinations out in September. Every year they said it, and as far as I know, there wasn't a kid in the school who didn't know how to get into all his friends' lockers.

I heard the numbers click and I opened the door. B.J.'s locker was a wreck. It always was, as if he lived in it. I expected to see breakfast dishes. I pushed back the papers that spilled out onto the floor and began looking for the letter. I wasn't sure that it would be there, but I hoped it would. B.J. hadn't had the letter with him the day before, so I

assumed that he had stashed it in his locker somewhere. I suspected that he'd want it on hand.

First I checked his coat pockets, but there wasn't
anything there but a couple of candy wrappers and
a paper clip. Then I started going through the papers on the shelf. God, there were old tests and
homework assignments that went all the way back
to September.

Finally, I did find it. The letter was folded neatly
inside an old notebook.

I tucked the letter under my arm and swung the
locker door closed. The sound of the metal slamming rang down the empty hall. No one was supposed to be in the corridors after twelve-fifteen.

I ran back toward Mr. Patterson's room. I wasn't
sure what was going to happen exactly. I was hoping that he would already have left for lunch and
that the room would be empty. That way I could
just put the letter on his desk where he would find
it later or slide it in under the door if the room
was locked. That would have been the easy way out.

But the door was open and Mr. Patterson was
sitting at his desk, looking over a pile of papers. I
knew that all the possible dialogues I had worked
out in my head all morning long wouldn't happen.

I walked in and stood at the door. Mr. Patterson looked up.

"Yes, Chad? Can I do something for you?"

"I've got something," I said. "I'd like to return
it."

I crossed the room. He folded his hands on the
blotter in front of him. I could see that his nails
were chewed down so far that they bled around
the edges. I hadn't noticed that before. I placed

142

the letter on the desk. Mr. Patterson looked at it and then back at me. A red flush crossed his face.

"I wanted to make sure that you got this back," I said.

He made a movement to rise and I backed up a step away from the desk. Then he sat back down and stayed in his seat.

"Were you doing this to me, Chad?"

"I'm sorry," I said. "It started as a joke. I never meant it to go this far."

"I ought to have your head for this."

"I know."

"Who else?" he asked.

"It doesn't matter. It's all over. I promise. I hope no real harm has been done. There aren't any more copies of the letter."

"You won't tell me who else?"

"No. I can't do that."

"Are they worth protecting?"

"I don't know."

"I think I know."

I nodded. He probably did.

Then he looked away, down at his hands. His eyes were all filled up. I was afraid he was going to cry or something. His fingers drummed on the desk blotter. I didn't know what else to do or say. I hoped he would yell at me or hit me. I think it would have made me feel a whole lot better. Right then, I felt like shit.

He looked up at me again. "I thank you for returning it."

"I wish I'd never seen it in the first place."

"So do I, Chad. It brought up memories I thought I'd left behind me." He gave a small smile. "Like you said in class, all good things have to end."

"I don't understand," I said. I didn't.

"You don't need to. You know about the Navy mess. The rest of my life history wouldn't interest you. The Navy wasn't the first time that things have not worked out and I suppose it won't be the last."

"Well, teaching's working out, isn't it? I mean, you're really a good teacher. We've all learned a lot from you this year. You can't let this whole mess get to you. Please, you can't take it personally. It was just a joke." I wasn't even convincing myself.

"I appreciate the sentiment, Chad, but it's a little late now. You're being very naïve."

"I'm sorry. I said I was sorry."

Then he looked up at me again and our eyes met.

"Do you think I'm crazy, Chad?"

"No, sir. I think you're less crazy than I am maybe. You make more sense anyway. Not much is making sense to me these days."

"I can understand that. I appreciate what you've done, Chad. It couldn't have been easy."

"I'd do it again. Now I would."

I turned away from him and walked back across the room. I went through the door and closed it behind me. I started down the stairs from the third floor.

I still felt rotten and sad. I had thought that returning the letter would make me feel better, but I guess things don't work that way. And now I had to tell B.J. and Toad what I had done and I didn't think that would be any easier. God, I felt trapped.

But not yet. I didn't want to face them right away.

Just as I got to the first floor, I saw Toad and

B.J. coming up from the commons. They spotted me at the same instant.

As I watched them coming up the hall toward me. I still couldn't decide whether I should confess right then and get it over with or just pretend, for the moment, that nothing had happened.

When they reached me they stopped, not saying anything. They just stood there in front of me, staring me down. We were standing by the double doors to the auditorium and suddenly B.J. grabbed the handle on one of the doors and yanked it open while Toad shoved me through the open space into the darkness.

I stumbled down the four steps just inside the door and caught my balance at the bottom. By then, the door was closed again and Toad and B.J. were standing on the step above, glaring down at me.

The auditorium was dim and quiet. I could hear our heavy breathing in the stillness. The sounds the rest of the school made seemed muffled and distant.

"What's going on?" I said. My voice was swallowed by the huge spaces of the auditorium.

"The letter's gone," B.J. said.

"Yeah."

"Do you know what happened to the letter?" B.J. asked. I felt his hot breath on my forehead. He couldn't have been more than a foot away, leaning down into my face.

"Yes." I took a step backward. "I took it out of your locker. I gave it back to Mr. Patterson."

"What the hell for?"

"Because we didn't have any right to it. We

didn't have any right to read it in the first place. The whole thing had gone far enough."

"And you decided that on your own?"

"But we were in this together, Chad," Toad said. "You shouldn't have done that. Now you've wrecked everything." His voice sounded watery and sad and lost in the big space.

"It was too mean. I thought this whole thing started as a joke, just for the fun of it. Don't you remember that? It didn't end up the way it started."

"It sure as hell didn't," B.J. said. "Toad's right. We agreed to stay in this thing together."

"Mr. Patterson doesn't know it was you. I didn't tell him. He only knows it was me. He won't tell anyone about it. I'm sure he won't. Who would he tell? He didn't deserve what we gave him." I glanced down. I couldn't stand his staring any longer.

B.J. reached down from the step above me and grabbed my hair, yanking my head back up. I jerked back in pain and surprise.

"Like hell," B.J. said.

"We should have voted on it," Toad said. "It was almost over anyway. Today was going to be the last day."

It was my turn to react. I laughed. "God, Toad, you don't really believe that, do you? You think this has been a democracy? Do you think those votes we had meant a goddamn thing?"

"Shut up," B.J. yelled. "Chad wouldn't have voted, Toad. He thinks he's better than we are. He thinks he can make it on his own."

"Listen, B.J., you and Toad wrote that other blackmail note without asking me. What about that, huh?"

"Shut your face up, Chad. It was two out of three, wasn't it?" He was really shouting now. "Wasn't it?" I could feel his spit in my face. "All for one and one for all? And you're so pure and innocent, you had to take things into your own hands."

"I'm glad I did," I yelled back.

"You know what you are, Chad Winston?" B.J.'s voice was cold and quiet again.

"What?"

"A goddamn traitor, a piece of shit. That's what you are. Well, you can believe me, it's still not over."

B.J. turned and started up the steps to the doors. Toad began to turn too.

"Toad," I said. "Toad, don't you go too."

But he did.

Both of them went up the stairs and through the doors and the doors shut solidly behind them. I was alone in the auditorium. I waited in the dark until the end of the lunch period. I was angry and sad. It had started out being so much fun. It wasn't supposed to happen like this.

When the bell rang, I steeled myself and walked back out into the busy hallway, all the unknowing faces rushing past to lockers and classrooms, talking about dumb stuff, unimportant stuff. No one knew what was going on inside my head, and there wasn't anyone else to share it with.

When I got to science class, I went on in and took my seat. No waiting in the halls. I kept half turning to look behind me, watching for B.J. and Toad to enter. But the bell to begin class rang and Mr. Feinster started talking and their seats were

147

still empty. They were cutting. All period I wondered why.

They weren't in history either. That surprised me even more. We were having a quiz and although maybe B.J. didn't really care about the grade, Toad usually did. Grades were too much like a game for him to take them lightly. If they were lucky, neither of the teachers would take roll and Toad and B.J. would get away with it. I didn't know why I was worried about them, for God's sake.

The three o'clock bell rang and I went out into the hall. I thought about skipping going to my locker, but I couldn't. I needed my math book. My locker was only about ten feet from Mr. Patterson's room, just across the corridor. I didn't want to see him again. I didn't want to run into Toad or B.J. either. All I wanted to do was get out of school and hurry home, safe and sound. Jesus, I couldn't even take my own good time getting my books organized anymore. That made me mad too.

I was just getting my stuff out of my locker, when I sensed someone standing behind me. I turned. It was B.J. I turned back to my locker.

"Hey, Chad, I'm sorry about what happened at lunch," he said.

I packed my books under my arm and started to leave, but B.J. stood in my way and wouldn't move.

"Listen, don't rush off. I want to apologize." He grinned and breathed in my face. "I shouldn't have blown my top. I was just disappointed, was all. I mean, you taking things into your own hands and all. I guess I hated to see it all end. Some of it was fun anyway."

"I'm not sorry I returned the letter," I said.

"I don't blame you. You were right. I just didn't realize how rotten we were being to Patterson. He's not such a bad guy. We got a little carried away, huh?"

"Yeah, you might say that."

The halls were emptying. There were a few last students slamming their locker doors.

"Anyway, I just wanted to tell you that I'm sorry I yelled and everything. Toad and I spent the last two periods talking about it. We agreed that you were right."

"Maybe we shouldn't be standing here outside Mr. Patterson's room," I said. "He still doesn't know who else was in on it but me."

"Oh, who the hell cares. It doesn't make any difference anymore. He can't really do anything."

"I guess not. I hope he doesn't take it out on me on the report card."

"He wouldn't do that. He wouldn't dare," B.J. said. His voice was still a little hard, not the same voice of just a week before. I had a feeling that his sense of power hadn't totally disappeared.

"Well, I've got to be heading off. Got to be home early today," I said.

"Why? What's on? I thought maybe you and Toad and I could go up to Gino's for a burger or something. Celebrate the end of our life of crime. Just for a few laughs, again, you know."

B.J. put his hands in his pockets and leaned against the row of lockers.

"Not today, thanks. I've got to get home."

"Are you still pissed, Chad? Don't be, huh? I said I was sorry, after all."

"No I'm not mad. I just have to get on home."

"Why? What's up?" Even then he was still pushing.

I tried to think of a quick answer but nothing came. I glanced down the hall to the staircase. The halls were empty.

"Nothing. My sister's birthday."

B.J. nodded. He stood up straight again, his hands still in his pockets.

I heard voices coming up the stairway from the end of the hall. One of the voices was Toad's.

"Well, don't stay mad at us, huh? All for one and one for all." B.J. grinned again. It wasn't his usual smile.

Toad appeared at the end of the hallway. Mr. Boughman, the assistant principal in charge of discipline, was with him. They started down the hall toward us. Mr. Boughman was looking down at Toad who as explaining something, his hands moving in erratic circles.

"I just thought you should know, Mr. Boughman. I don't usually like to squeal on other students, but this is pretty serious as far as I can see," I heard Toad say.

"You're right, Toad. I appreciate your coming to me." Mr. Boughman looked up. "There he is now."

I glanced again at B.J. I didn't understand what was going on. Had they told Mr. Boughman about our blackmail letters?

"Listen, chum, we'll be seeing you later," B.J. said quickly and walked away in the opposite direction of Toad and Mr. Boughman.

"I didn't think he'd still be here, Mr. Boughman. I shouldn't have come along."

"It's best that he is," Mr. Boughman said.

I started to close my locker, but Mr. Boughman

yelled down the hall, "Leave that locker open, Winston."

I froze and then turned back toward them. As I did, I glanced down. Lying next to my feet, on the yellow carpet, were three poorly rolled, homemade cigarettes.

I looked back up at Mr. Boughman. He was almost next to me by then. He had seen them too. Toad hung back, about ten feet behind.

I looked down at my feet again. The three reefers were still there. Amazingly they hadn't disappeared. Even my wishing had made no difference. Then I knew why B.J.'s hands had been in his pockets. I could guess at the hole that led into his pant's leg and the way he had let the three marijuana joints slide quietly out onto the floor in front of my locker.

Mr. Boughman reached over and picked them up. He held them cupped in his hand as he moved them up toward his face. I could hear him inhale deeply.

"That's not tobacco," he said. "Is it, Chad?"

"I wouldn't know," I said. "I don't smoke."

I saw Toad turn and walk quietly toward the stairs. Mr. Boughman didn't bother to notice. At the stairway door, Toad looked back. At least he appeared to be miserable. That was something anyway.

"I don't suppose they fell out of your locker either?" Mr. Boughman said.

"No, sir, they didn't. Somebody must have dropped them on the floor. I didn't even notice them until you came along."

"Your parents know you blow grass?" Mr. Boughman asked.

"I don't."

Mr. Boughman gave a short snort. "Just appeared out of nowhere on the floor where you're standing? No one else in sight? Strange coincidence, don't you think?"

"Not so strange. It happened, didn't it. You never saw me with them. You never even saw me touch them. Fifteen minutes ago this hall was crawling with kids."

Mr. Boughman began raising his voice. He was big on Gestapo tactics. "Bull, Winston. I got a report that there was grass in your locker. And you're asking me to believe that these just happened to appear out of thin air? You're asking me to believe that?"

Then Mr. Patterson was at the door of his room. There was a strange, weary expression on his face.

"Believe it, Boughman," Mr. Patterson said. "Believe it, because it's true. Those joints are mine."

Mr. Boughman looked incredulous. "Now, wait a minute, Jim. . . ."

"You heard what I said. Chad Winston's got nothing to do with those marijuana cigarettes. They're mine. I must have dropped them by mistake."

"Oh, come on, Jim," Mr. Boughman started to say, "You're not really asking me to believe. . . ."

"I'm not asking anything. I don't care what you believe. I'm telling you that those are mine. It's what I say that counts. You don't have any choice."

"That's crazy, Jim. Why would you say a thing like that? I tell you, I won't believe it."

"That doesn't matter at all. You can't blame Chad now."

Mr. Patterson reached out his hand.

"I'll keep these if you don't mind," Mr. Bough-man said.

Mr. Patterson pulled back his hand.

"As you wish. Chad, go on home," Mr. Patterson said.

I looked at Mr. Patterson. He was standing there with his arms thrust out from his sides, palms up. His face was the saddest face I'd ever seen, filled with terrible knowledge of good things lost.

I hesitated. I didn't want to leave him.

"Did you hear me?" Mr. Patterson yelled. "Get the hell out of here. It's over."

I slammed the locker door closed and made it to the stairs before the sound of the banging door stopped echoing in the hall.

CHAPTER 8

When I got to English the next day, I went right to
my seat and stared straight ahead, looking at the
woman sitting behind Mr. Patterson's desk. She was
thin and had graying hair and a pair of glasses
hanging from her neck by one of those chain things.

Even when B.J. came in and took his seat, right
beside me, I continued gazing only in front. There
was considerable buzzing from the class around me.
When everyone was in and seated, the woman rose
from her chair and walked to the center of the
front of the room. She seemed out of place behind
Mr. Patterson's homemade podium.

The class quieted.

"Good morning. My name is Mrs. Evershaw. I'll
be your English teacher for the rest of the year.
Now, I know it will be. . . ."

LeeAnne raised her hand.

"Yes, dear? What is it?"

"Well, Mrs. Evershaw, where's Mr. Patterson? Is
he sick?"

"I don't really know for sure, dear. All I can
tell you is that the school district has hired me for
the duration of the year." She smiled. "Now I un-

derstand that you've been studying some English literature."

B.J. leaned over toward my desk. "Hey, Chad, what do you think of that?"

I glanced at him. I felt like wiping that smile off his face with a sledgehammer.

"What did I tell you," B.J. said. "The perfect crime, huh? We got rid of him, didn't we?"

For just a moment I wondered how much of everything that had happened had been planned.

"Young man," Mrs. Evershaw said. "Please don't talk while I'm talking."

B.J. started to laugh.

"Young man," Mrs. Evershaw said again. "I've asked you not to speak out of turn. I don't understand what you find so amusing. What is your name?"

B.J. looked at her and gave a slight bow of his head. "Chad Winston, ma'am."

There was laughter from the rest of the class.

"I'm Chad Winston," I said.

"We'll see. We shall see," she said and continued with the lesson, Shakespeare's *All's Well That Ends Well*.

Obviously *Paradise Lost* was gone with Mr. Patterson.

Mrs. Evershaw droned on for the rest of the period about the structure of Elizabethan society and the whole class drifted into a state of stupor. The boredom was only broken by B.J.'s constant interruptions and supposedly humorous asides, until finally, Mrs. Evershaw sent him into the hall for the remainder of the period. I was already realizing how much I was going to miss Mr. Patterson and his somewhat eccentric approach to English literature.

"I want you all to read the first four scenes for tomorrow. We'll have a quiz so you'll want to be sure to do a careful reading."

The class groaned and the bell rang.

When I reached the hall, B.J. and Toad were waiting for me. They were laughing together, as if they were planning new plots and strategies.

I turned in the opposite direction and began to make my way through the crowds. I only got a few feet before I felt B.J.'s arm thrown around my shoulder. Toad materialized on the other side.

"Jesus, what an old goat she is," B.J. said. "Give us a week and we'll have her begging for mercy."

I pulled away from them, shaking B.J.'s arm off my shoulder. I didn't want him touching me.

"What the hell's the matter with you?" he said.

I couldn't hold it in any longer.

"What the hell's the matter with me?" I said. "After what you tried to do to me yesterday, you're wondering why I'm not exactly happy to see you?"

"Oh, come on. What's with you, huh? Jeez, Chad, it was just a little joke."

"Right. A little joke. Well, all of a sudden I think your sense of humor stinks. That little joke could have gotten me thrown out of school."

"Hey, Chad," Toad said. "We were just messing around. You know, to get you back for taking the letter. It didn't mean anything."

"And the fact that Mr. Patterson is gone for good doesn't give your conscience even a little twinge?"

"Patterson? Hell, you were in on that. He deserved it, didn't he?"

"No," I said. "Nobody deserves what we did."

B.J. shrugged.

"Let's get on down to lunch," Toad said. "I'm starved. Sorry about yesterday."

He turned toward the staircase and B.J. started to follow. I didn't move.

They got about five paces and stopped. B.J. turned back toward me. "Coming?" he said.

"No."

"Don't you think you're taking this a little seriously?"

"No."

"Well, listen, kid, when you get tired of sulking by yourself, let us know." He flashed me a smile. "There's always the movies on Friday night."

B.J. punched Toad in the arm. It must have hurt because Toad frowned and started rubbing the spot.

"Come on, Toad. Let the bastard stew. He'll come crawling back when he decides he needs a friend or two."

They pushed the stair doors open and started down, two steps at a time.

I stayed away from the two of them all that week and the next. I ignored them during class and avoided them at lunch and in the halls. Toad called me once at home, but my sister answered and I told her to tell him I was at the town library.

I was plenty lonely and I almost went over to their table at lunch a couple of times but I didn't. I figured the loneliness would do me good, a little penance for my guilt, so to speak.

What bothered me more than the loss of my friendship with Toad and B.J. was wondering what had happened to Mr. Patterson. As far as I knew, he had just disappeared from the earth. The week after it all had happened there was a notice in the local paper that the school board had accepted the resignation of Mr. Patterson, but it didn't say anything else. Nothing about where he might be going.

Winter warmed and by the end of March the snow was long gone and there were buds on the trees, waiting for the first really warm day to turn themselves into leaves. One Monday morning Miss vanderPoole, the English teacher, stopped me in the hall.

"Chad Winston, right?" she said.

"Yes."

"Well, I got a letter from Jim Patterson on Saturday and he made a point in it to have me say hello to you from him. He sends his best."

Just hearing that made me feel better.

"Thanks, Miss vanderPoole. Where is he? Did he say?"

"Oh, sure. He's teaching in a small private school in New Hampshire. Says he likes it very much."

"That's good," I said. "Could I possibly have his address?"

"I don't see why not. It's Carleton Hill Academy, Carleton, New Hampshire."

"Thanks, Miss vanderPoole. Thanks a lot."

"Well, sure. See you later, Chad."

I watched her go down the hall. I pulled a piece of paper out of my notebook and jotted down the address before I forgot it. I knew I wanted to write Mr. Patterson a letter, that things wouldn't be really over until I apologized one more time.

I sat at my desk that night with a pile of stationery in front of me. It wasn't easy to write, that letter. I knew what I wanted to express, but I didn't know how to put it into words. I wanted to apologize. I also wanted to thank Mr. Patterson. It ended up being harder to say "Thank You" than "I'm Sorry," harder to express my gratitude than guilt. Anyway, it took me a long time. When I was done, I read it back over, mostly pleased with what I had said.

Dear Mr. Patterson,

I hope you don't mind if I wrote you a letter. You can throw it out if you want. Miss vanderPoole gave me your address. I asked her for it. There were a few things I wanted to say.

I hope you like your new school. Your students are lucky. We ended up with a boring old lady who took your place. She makes everything very boring.

I don't really know why you resigned, whether Mr. Boughman forced you to because of the marijuana cigarettes, or whether you had already decided to. But either way, I figure it's my fault and I just wanted to say I was sorry the whole thing happened. It doesn't do any good now, I guess, but I am sorry and if I could take everything back and make it last January again, I would. I feel about as dumb and awful as anyone could.

It wasn't my joints that were on the floor outside of the locker. I figure that maybe you already know that, although it doesn't make any difference. Toad and B.J. planted them there to get back at me for returning the letter. They were in on the whole letter plot from the beginning, although I'm not trying to get out of the blame. They'd probably kill me if they knew I was telling you this, but I really don't care. I want you to know. Besides, Toad and B.J. aren't my friends anymore. I don't know whether they've changed or I have, but everything they do now seems pretty dumb, so I just haven't been hanging around with them anymore lately.

There's one other thing I want to tell you and that is that I really appreciate all you did for me. And I don't mean just taking the blame that afternoon. I mean about all kinds of things, like for being such a good teacher and not smashing my head in when I returned the letter and things like that. Mostly though, I want to thank you because I think you've made me see things in a new way. I think that if I've been the one to change around here, that you had a lot to do with it. And I'm sorry that you're not around anymore because I miss talking with you.

Anyway, I hope your new school is great and that you get treated better there than we treated you here. I mean it when I say you were one of the best teachers I ever had. I hope you're happy and good luck for the future.

Sincerely,
Chad Winston

I felt better after I mailed it. It settled my mind down to have put my apology in black and white, and made my feelings official and known to Mr. Patterson.

I was surprised a few days later when I got home

from school and my mother told me there was a letter for me. It was lying on the radiator cover in the front hall along with *Time* magazine and a couple of advertisements.

I picked it up and glanced at the return address on the back. It was from Mr. Patterson. I stuck it in my notebook and started upstairs.

"Who's it from?" my mother asked, although I figure she already had looked at the return address.

"From Mr. Patterson," I said. "My old English teacher."

"The one that left so suddenly?"

"Yeah," I said. "He's teaching up in New England now."

"That was nice of him to write."

"Yeah. He probably needs some help in analyzing *Hamlet* and wants my advice," I said.

Mom laughed.

"I'll be upstairs if you want me for anything."

"Fine."

I went on up the stairs. I could feel my mother watching me as I turned at the landing and disappeared from her view.

I threw the books down on my bed and ripped the envelope open. I pulled the letter out, sprawled out on my back on top of the bedspread, and began to read.

Dear Chad,

I just received your letter this morning and I'm writing back immediately. I know it must not have been easy for you to write but it expresses your feelings very well. It would have been easy for you to have shut the door on the incident, pushed a chair over to brace against the knob, and hoped that the door would stay shut for the rest of your life. But take my word for it, from someone who has several of those doors all jammed shut, they have a strange way of creaking open when you least expect them to, and unpleasant memories have an unfortunate way of oozing through the cracks. So not only was your letter a thoughtful thing to do for me, but I suspect, in the long run, that it will do you some benefit as well.

I like Carleton Hill quite well. After just a few months here, I feel comfortable. The school is small and the atmosphere relaxed. So far the school seems to be adjusting to me as readily as I am adjusting to it. Besides teaching English, I am a dorm master, drama sponsor, and will coach a soccer team next fall. It may well be I have finally found my niche and will settle down and spend the next fifty years slowly metamorphosing into Mr. Chips.

When you mentioned that your friendships with Toad and B.J. had faded, I was not particularly surprised. I had already assumed that they were your cohorts. It was not hard to surmise. You were quite inseparable throughout the fall and winter. However, Chad, I could observe you maturing much faster than the other two. Although this must seem little consolation to you now as they laugh and plan new plots, very few friendships are permanent. New ones seem to arrive just when you need them the most. Things will get better. That's the voice of experience speaking.

Again, thank you for your thoughtful letter. It was a pleasure knowing you, believe it or not.

> Sincerely,
> Jim Patterson

It's funny. I appreciated Mr. Patterson's letter, but it was depressing in a way too. It made me realize again how completely things had changed. I mean, in just three or four months, nothing was the same at all. I used to be comfortable and secure, and now I was starting from scratch all over again.

It was good to have the letter anyway. I was glad to know that Mr. Patterson was happy. It was easy picturing him at Carleton Hill, sliding into the routine and becoming an integral part of that little world. I almost wished I was up there with him, insulated from the outside, but accepted into a system larger than myself.

I stayed sprawled out on the bed for a while, until Mom called me for dinner, imagining myself at a desk in a small, wooden-paneled room, listening to Mr. Patterson expound dramatically about some piece of classic English literature.

CHAPTER 9

I didn't realize how much Mr. Patterson's letter had affected me until today in school when I saw Toad and B.J. together before homeroom. They were standing in the hall outside the door, chuckling insanely over something, and for the first time I didn't even wonder what it was.

B.J. spotted me and yelled, "Hey, Chad, baby, come on over here for a second."

I hesitated and then walked over to them.

"Yeah?" I said.

"We got something to show you. Just for old times' sake," B.J. said. He reached into his pocket and pulled out an envelope. He held it toward me, but I didn't take it. I could see that Mrs. Evershaw's name was written on the outside.

"Last night's reading assignment gave me the idea," he said.

"What about it?" I asked. We were finishing the year in English by studying *The Canterbury Tales,* English literature in reverse chronological order for some strange reason. The whole class had read the Prologue together and then Mrs. Evershaw had assigned us all to choose one of the tales to read. I'd read The Pardoner's Tale.

"I read The Miller's Tale last night. Jeez, is it raunchy. The miller is messing around with the reeve's wife and the reeve ends up shoving a hot poker up the poor guy's ass."

"Sounds like a story you'd enjoy," I said.

"Well, it grossed out my poor virginal ears, I can tell you that. And—well, you know how much I love to write letters. I couldn't resist the opportunity."

He shoved the letter toward me again.

"Aren't you curious?" B.J. asked. "Go ahead. It won't bite."

I shrugged and took it.

"Well, open it."

I pulled out a single sheet of paper and read it:

Dear Mrs. Evershaw,

I was appalled to discover that you had assigned my son to read a piece of obscenity like the Miller's Tale. The fact that a written work is old does not mean that it is suitable for young readers. I had assumed that a person in a position of responsibility would exercise enough sense not to deliberately corrupt the minds of our township's students. I am addressing copies of this letter to both your principal and the superintendent, with additional copies going to the school board. I hope you will be able to justify your actions to them.

Sincerely,
Mrs. Benjamin Masterson

"We're not really sending copies to the school board," Toad said.

"Pretty well written, isn't it?" B.J. said. "I figure it'll hit her where it hurts."

I handed it back to B.J. He looked surprised.

"Aren't you going to rip it up?" B.J. said.

"No. I figure you've probably got another copy in your notebook."

B.J. threw his head back and laughed.

"I tell you, Winston. You may be an asshole, but you're not a dumb asshole."

He stuffed the letter back into its envelope and stuck it into his notebook.

"I just want you to know something. For old times' sake," I said.

B.J. was still laughing. "Oh, yeah? What?"

"I wouldn't give her that letter if I were you."

"And why not?"

"Because Mr. Patterson is going to press charges of blackmail against you and it wouldn't be real bright to make it any worse than it is."

The grin left B.J.'s face. Toad stepped back against the wall.

B.J. cocked one eyebrow up. "Come on. Don't give me any of that shit."

"I'm not kidding you, B.J."

"You're out of your head. He's gone. He wouldn't do anything like that."

"Sure he would. What's he got to lose? He can't exactly be fired anymore, can he?"

"You're just messing around, aren't you, Chad?" Toad said.

"Jesus," B.J. said. "It would be just like someone as rotten as Patterson to pull a trick like that. Jesus."

"Yeah? Well, anyway, I think I'd burn that letter to Mrs. Evershaw, if I were you. No sense pushing your luck."

"I don't believe you," B.J. said.

"So don't believe me. It's your grave. So dig it."

"Come on, now. You're kidding, aren't you?"

For the first time I gave B.J. and Toad a big smile. I turned away from them, and entered the classroom on my own.

ABOUT THE AUTHOR

CHARLES P. CRAWFORD grew up in Wayne, Pennsylvania. He attended Williams College and later earned an M.A.T. from Johns Hopkins University. He is now a teacher at Radnor Township School District in Wayne. Mr. Crawford is married and has a young son named Chad.

Although the characters and events in *Letter Perfect* are fictional, they come out of an environment that the author knows well, and they reflect his deep interest in the shifting loyalties of teen-age friendships and the effect of peer pressure on certain kinds of students.

Mr. Crawford is the author of two other books for young adults, *Bad Fall* and *Three-Legged Race*.